LOUISÀ

LOUISÀ

Dear Trista —
I wish you a lifetime
of happiness and adventure —
always trust in God — He is
your best friend —
Love
Grandma Louise
7/28/18

LOUISE LANGFORD

Library of Congress Control Number:		2015912206
ISBN:	Hardcover	978-1-5035-9135-6
	Softcover	978-1-5035-9134-9
	eBook	978-1-5035-9133-2

Print information available on the last page.

Rev. date: 08/10/2015

To order additional copies of this book, contact:
Xlibris
1-888-795-4274
www.Xlibris.com
Orders@Xlibris.com
715849

CONTENTS

For my grandchildren

AUTHOR'S NOTE

The places, names, and circumstances I have entered here are as factual and close to what I saw and heard as I can remember.

I suppose this writing would fall under the term *memoirs*. To me, that sounds rather stuffy and dull. I would think of it, rather, as an accounting—an accounting to my grandchildren for those seventeen years they spent without me, to my fellow Central Montanans and my church for their unquestioning faith and support during both normal times and the disasters, and to my children, without whom I could never have "stayed the course."

It is an accounting for me as well, a reminder that when I sit back and think "Why didn't I?" or "If only I had," I can rest assured that I did the best I could, with whatever tools I had, and made the best decisions possible.

It is so titled because, for whatever else it may be, it
is a love story . . . and he called her *Louisà*.

FOREWORD

I have agonized over documenting my time in Honduras. Years have passed, and old griefs have healed. Now it is time, time to pass on what I lived and learned to you, my grandchildren—the generation I missed.

I wasn't here to share your joys and challenges. You had my heart; however, my mind and body were far away, not in miles, but in a world you could never imagine. I knew you were all safe and loved, yet day after day I stood with children who weren't—whose greatest hope was food, a hug, for some little friends to kick a bottle cap back and forth with. Or maybe the wistful look of a little girl, with the family's new baby riding on her hip as she watched her mom hanging the wash on the fence to dry in that glorious hot sun, the jeans always turned inside out to dry the pockets and save the color.

Eyes tell so much. Sometimes they were bright and snappy at the sight of a moving bug, or maybe spotting a little snake, which always brought the adults. Snakes were bad. Even so, children always found something to be happy about, and that makes life livable.

There were others—the sad, frantic eyes of a young mother on a side street in the city, her newborn breathing its last breath. She shoved it in front of me begging for *dinero* for *medicina*. I immediately gave all I had, which was instantly snatched by a man smelling of booze, who had somehow materialized from the alley. I screamed and called for help as the distraught woman and what I was sure was an almost-dead infant also disappeared into the same alley.

I stumbled the half block to Hernandez Drug in that hot, burning midday sun, calling for my friend Hermione, the owner. People stared silently as I blurted out my story. She came around the counter and took my arm. Tears streamed down my cheeks. Her soft words stayed with me through the years. "Mrs. Langford, we do what we can. There is nothing more you can do. The baby is much better with his Lord. He never would have lived. You cannot let yourself get so upset. You do what you can and pray to God to watch over these little ones."

Hermione saw me through many bad times. She was a good person, gracious, deeply religious, her graying hair pulled back into a bun, and spoke excellent English. She had been a doctor who gave up her practice and now ran the *farmacia*, Hernandez Drug.

There were the blank, dead eyes of a little four-year-old, small for her age, with long, stringy black hair and a faded gray shift that hung from her skinny little frame. When I drove up to the house, a lean-to with plastic hung to form a windbreak, she was trying to scrape some food from the bottom of a cooking pan with a worn-down metal spoon and, from the sound, not getting much.

She looked at me with those eyes, and as my friend Jean talked in rapid Spanish to her pregnant mother, I took a little plastic doll, a real cheapie packaged in cellophane, and held it out to her. She hesitated, then reached out and took it quickly, before I changed my mind, and folded it to her little breast with both arms. When she looked up at me, her eyes sparkled. There were gifts for the others, and food, but she was special. As I drove away, she was standing, watching me, smiling, the cellophane still on the doll clasped tightly to her chest.

I am telling you this because, with all we have, it is hard to realize how these things can happen and even be so close.

When I left to teach what I thought would be that one year in Honduras and heard the plane door close in Sheridan, I remembered the tears in Candy's eyes and Cindy's half-joking, emotional words on the phone, "I just know they're going to cook you and eat you." Even though I would smile at that thought, I still heard the worry in her voice.

Moms don't do that. We aren't supposed to go traipsing off to some faraway place, but I did. And from the time I left, as I watched them seal my bags, and as I looked out my plane window at that frighteningly immense span of water, I began a conversation with God that has never ended. He was my guide, my mentor, my friend. He was all I had, and as I learned through the coming years, He was all I needed.

* * * * * *

I often sit and think of the children and the orphans in the *guardaria*. The day after Hurricane Mitch ended its six-day desecration of Honduras, it was still raining, cold, and so wet. Everything was soaked. Someone said I should probably check the guardaria. I didn't know what that was. Then they said "*niños*," and I went. *Guardaria* was the Spanish term for "orphanage."

It was an old building. The paint had almost totally worn off. A Catholic sister in a white habit let me in and waved her hand at the roomful of children. There were at least thirty, ranging from infants to twelve-year-olds. They had been rescued from the water, dragged from collapsed buildings, brought in from the mountains, anywhere and everywhere—all without family, love, hope, or food.

They sat, unsmiling, and watched me. I tried to talk to them, but whether it was my accent, my strangeness, whatever, they did not answer. Finally, some began fiddling with my hair. They tried to open my purse, played with my watch and rings, and began to laugh among themselves. Children recover so quickly. They covered their hopelessness with the here and now, which is how their parents had lived every day.

One boy, about eleven, would not talk. He just stared off into space. Eduardo. I asked the sister if they had eaten. She smiled. "We have no food, Teacher." I left to see what I could find.

Everyone in Honduras was trying to get food. I went to a vendor I knew; I had his daughter in my class. Throngs were five deep in front of his *pulperìa*.[1] I thought, *Dear God*. He looked up at me, jerked his head

---

[1]   general store

to the back, and I drove around and parked. I told him why I needed food. He answered quickly, "Teacher, we have no more food. But one moment, I will see what I can do." He disappeared for a few moments then came out carrying several large sacks. I paid double, but I had food.

Back in the guardaria, the excited sisters explained they had no cooking gas. The *chimbras* had run out. So back to the lines and with the same result.

I said good-bye to the children and went to check on other refugees they were bringing in to the schools. A barge was unloading—old women, babies, young mothers, children—all staring at nothing, like small zombies, blank faces void of all expression. I put my hand on the old woman's arm. She looked through me as though in a trance and walked ahead.

Carlos Diaz, a student of mine who had brought the barge in with his father, told me they had plucked these folks from the trees, where they had hung for days. Those who fell were swept away in the current, and the ones lucky enough to stay in the trees found themselves victims of hungry ants and snakes, also trying to survive. Their little legs and bodies were masses of bites and stings.

Dr. Christina Rodriguez, another of my students' mothers and also a friend, asked if I would transport these *damnificados*[2] to the clinic to be treated. I had a topper on the back of my pickup. We packed it full of miserable human beings for the hot half-mile ride to the clinic. Later, they were brought back outside, their bites covered with purple medicine, and again loaded into the back of the pickup to be taken to the schools for food and a place to sleep.

As I was sitting on a pile of rubble from a crumbled wall, waiting for yet another load of refugees to be treated, I wrote a letter home. Candy put the letter in the *Lewistown News-Argus*, and contributions from all over Central Montana poured in. Home, which had seemed so far away, was suddenly within reach. Thankfulness, love, and appreciation flooded through me.

---

2   homeless

I saw one of the sisters from the guardaria on the street a few weeks later. "I wish you had returned," she told me. "Eduardo stood by the gate for days waiting to see you." I too wished I had taken time to go back.

* * * * * *

Life is so delicate in the third world. Death is an everyday occurrence, and when it happens, you do what you can, help where you can, and learn to live each day to its fullest.

I first lived in a little barrio a block from the school, a room in Doña Lela's home. My friend Lupè lived on one side of us, and Doña Aurora on the other. The clinic, with Dr. Christina as director, covered the block between us and the school.

At six in the morning, as I made my way to the school gate, I passed the waiting room of this clinic. It was totally open, except for protective iron bars. Several huge old fans hung from the ceiling, rotating lazily to give a bit of relief to the heat, which was becoming very real.

By that time of the morning, it was packed full of at least sixty to seventy patients—each with their number, mostly mothers holding sick crying babies or children flushed with fever—all quietly waiting. I tried to smile sympathetically to them as I passed. Their eyes bespoke their longing; what it would be like to be a North American; rich, like they thought I must be, and able to do, say, or have the things they wanted.

And I, in turn, was impressed by their cleanliness. The clothes were worn but spotlessly clean from many sessions with the washboard—a daily part of the life of these devoted women who sat waiting, so patiently waiting for their number to come up, their turn to see the *doctora*.

Early one hot, humid morning, I was in my classroom, getting papers readied for the day, trying not to let the sweat that was dripping from my chin get on the sheets of paper. Someone came into my room and quietly told me that Lupè, who was a teacher's assistant, had lost her father, an ancient who lived with her. I ran to her house. The neighborhood ladies were all dutifully seated, as custom dictated, in her living room.

"Where is Lupè?"

They pointed upstairs, and I immediately started to climb the narrow steps.

"Teacher, no, you can't go up there. She is preparing him." I looked at them, smiled, and continued.

I found Lupè gently washing her father, tears rolling down her face. "I can't get his arms folded, Miss, and I have no box," she cried.

I looked at his arms. She had tried bending them. I had worked at funerals, playing the organ, and death was no stranger, but this was pretty close. I took his cold arm—like a board.

"What will I do?" She was sobbing.

"Here," I said, "help me." We twisted as hard as we could. It finally gave, just enough, a feeling I won't forget.

"How much is a box, Lupè?"

"I need six hundred *limps*, Miss. I have three hundred."

I pulled out a five-hundred lempira[3] bill, gave it to her, and she called her grandson to come upstairs. He and a friend returned in less than thirty minutes with a big black box. They loaded Lupè's father, now fully dressed, his arms crossed, and rolls of white cotton protruding from each nostril—again, the custom.

A final hug from her was my thank-you, which I passed on to my friend. I always talked about God to my students as my *friend*. He was part of me and every breath I drew.

During my years in Honduras, I skirted danger in so many places—mudslides, a hurricane, an earthquake, the beach, streets, snakes, robbers, guns, machetes, insects, diseases, and countless other ways. I

---

3   Honduran currency (ratio: 10 to 1 at that time)

must have been like a child led by an angel. I look back and think of the twenty-third psalm. I was there.

* * * * * *

My constant companion through these years of my life was my big old stuffed bear—a silent source of comfort and quiet wisdom, a reflection of my dreams, hopes, trials, and a sounding board when things became unbearable.

This is his story. He watched it unfold and saw what I could not. He's still with me. His nose is partly gone, his mouth has faded, and his fur isn't quite as plush. But then look at me—past eighty, gray (silver as I like to call it), wrinkled, and I don't walk as well or as fast as I used to. Nevertheless, it has been a life I would never have wanted to change; even the hard times, some of which still tear at my heart.

So listen, niños, for inside each of you are the same genes I carry. You can't deny them. That is why I know you will understand each word I am going to share with you. This is not the story you are expecting to hear, but it is of life—my life. . . and you were there with me.

God's grace.

CHAPTER 1

"Ladies and gentlemen, this is your captain speaking. May I please have your attention?"

It took a few seconds for the boisterous, eager-to-be-home group of men in the center-back of the plane to quiet down.

"As you undoubtedly noticed, we have circled the airport and are in position to land. Our landing gear is down. However, we are unable to confirm it has locked. I am sending my first officer down to check it out and, if necessary, lock it by hand. There is no cause for alarm. This should take only a few minutes. Thank you."

It was very quiet. Louise was seated on the left side of the aircraft, close to the front, in the window seat. This was the first leg of her trip back to the States to visit her children after another year of teaching in Tela, Honduras. Excited to be back in her country, she was looking forward to flights the next day to Denver, Billings, and home.

She had noticed the red lights flashing on the runways. *Hmm, some sort of problem down there,* she thought.

The young officer stepped into the cabin. His attempt at professional calm didn't cover his pale face. He moved quickly down the aisle and disappeared. When he failed to come back soon, edginess set in. The cabin remained quiet. As she looked out the window, she saw more and more flashing red lights, so tiny from above, but she could make out fire trucks, police, and what looked like ambulances.

Slowly, the pieces tumbled into place. The problem was this plane, the one she was on; the circling, the increasing lights below, the possibilities, and the helplessness all flooded her mind. She fought to bring some reason to what was happening. There was none.

The officer came hurriedly back through, looking straight ahead. The voice came through the intercom again, "Ladies and gentlemen, this is your captain. We believe we have the problem under control. However, to be safe, I want each of you to assume the position for an impact landing. This is only a preventative measure. The attendants will now instruct you. Please give them your full cooperation. Thank you."

"May I have your attention?" she spoke slowly and clearly. "At this time your seat belt should be fastened and your seat in an upright position. Now lean forward. Put your head as near your knees as possible, with your arms clasped over your head. Please stay in this position until we have safely landed. Thank you."

It was silent—dead silent. Seconds passed like hours.

Louise finally raised her head just enough to peek out the window. The tops of the pine trees lining the runway were flying by, then the whole tree. She quickly pulled her head back down. This was the moment, waiting for the thud and screech of the tires on the pavement.

When it came, each microsecond seemed an eternity. The afterburners roared in, and the force pulled at her body. The wheels held. Seconds later, they were still holding. As the plane slowed, heads came up. Still, not a sound. A quiet clap, soft, almost subdued, spread through the cabin, joined by all but hardly heard. Then again, the intense silence. No one looked around; no one spoke. Every soul knew they were a survivor, snatched from the grim fingers of disaster.

Suitcases came down; passengers moved out and down the aisle patiently, without a word.

Louise glanced at a few faces as they deplaned down the Jetway and out into the Houston terminal. There were no smiles, just silent, set faces. She wondered what they were thinking—of their families, of how unimportant that important business meeting they were headed to really was, or of their lives.

She headed for the immigration lines, more eager than ever to see her family. *Dear God, thank you.*

As she lay in her hotel bed that night, she backtracked through the day's events—more than that, the past year and the year before. She wondered, really wondered, *What am I doing here? Is this where I should be?* She talked with God, questions upon questions, agonized, argued, and thanked Him, finally dozing off.

Six weeks later, after a fulfilling visit with family, she flew out of Billings and headed back to Denver. There she boarded her flight for Houston en route to San Pedro Sula and Honduras. She was sitting next to a young woman in her late twenties or early thirties. During the conversation, she asked what type of work the woman did.

"I'm an air controller," she said.

"Where?"

"At Houston International."

"How exciting," said Louise. "I imagine you are always thankful when you get off shift without having any serious problems."

"Oh yes," the woman answered. "On my shift earlier this summer, we had a plane come in with landing gear that wouldn't lock. It was a bad situation. We really thought we were going to have a disaster, but somehow, it held. It was a pretty tense few minutes."

"I know," answered Louise. "I was on that plane. It was from San Pedro Sula."

Her new friend gave her a quick glance. "Yes."

Louise looked out the window, her mind wandering back to how her life had changed so totally in just a few years. Her friends were all home, baking cookies, babysitting grandchildren, running to Little League games or to school plays, and here she was, flying over the clouds to a far different world. It was hard to understand. She didn't know why; she only knew she was doing it.

She rested her head against the seat and closed her eyes, her mind slipping back through the years—those years when their life had been so trying, full of love, hand in hand with sadness, despair, and ultimately, the grief. It had been so final and so very hard; yet somehow, out of it all, she had found her way.

This is her story and mine. I watched her struggle, grieve, and survive.

My life with Louise began one day back in 1988 when her husband, Lennie, was still alive. I was sitting in a store window, marked down for a quick sale. I had one of those old-fashioned, realistic faces, not the sweet kind the new bears have; and I was pretty big, close to three feet high. When she looked through that window and saw me, she smiled, came into the store, and took me home. Louise never had a big, cuddly bear and put me on their bed, atop its puffy yellow comforter.

She and Lennie lived in a large four-bedroom home where they raised Lennie's three children and those of Louise's four who were still at home. Both had been married before. Life was busy with family, friends, and keeping their big garden and lawn.

There were many special times, busy times. Of all these, Louise loved Thanksgiving. Christmas always seemed so hurried; she usually played the organ for services at St. James Episcopal Church, but Thanksgiving was family day.

Early in the morning, Lennie got up, went to the kitchen, and soon the house was filled with "You Are My Sunshine" as he bathed the turkey. He washed it like a baby, every little fold and part, serenading it all the time, totally unaware that each member of the family was lying in bed listening. It was such a beautiful way to start the day.

Then he would gently dry the big bird, set it in the roaster to wait for the final touches, and make a cup of coffee. His part was done.

He was away most weeks during the summer, working construction. Weekends were spent with family. In the fall, he took the boys on hunting trips, but summer weekends meant fishing. He was never happier than when he was sitting in his canoe, out on the pond drowning a worm.

Lennie rode a big Yamaha 1500 road bike. The motorcycle was hit by a car at an intersection; he suffered several skull fractures. A year later, a stroke forced him to stop working. Doctors finally diagnosed him as having a terminal blood-clotting problem. He fought the disease for years. Louise talked to God a lot during that time. She knew the end was coming; she didn't want to lose him.

His last fishing trip was with his two brothers. He had gained a good amount of weight from the medicine he was taking. Moving him was hard. They got him into the canoe and pushed off. Lennie sat in the middle, Howard in front, and Clarence in the back. Howard baited Lennie's line, tossed it in the water, and handed him the rod.

Shortly, there was a tug on the line. Clarence helped him reel in the big trout, removed the hook, bagged the fish, and gave the line to Howard, who hooked up another plump nightcrawler. Then he placed it back in Lennie's hands.

Louise found an empty pill bottle while they were gone and knew he had secretly fortified himself. She smiled. It was worth it. He had not been this happy for months.

When Lennie died in 1993, she asked the guitarist to play his favorite song, "You Are My Sunshine," as the people filed out. They had been married twenty-two years. He was a wonderful big bear of a man—gentle, soft-spoken, and a good father who died much too early.

She held me tight and cried and cried.

On a warm spring afternoon in 1994, she was relaxing in her comfortable easy chair after working her dispatching shift at the sheriff's office. She wasn't really happy—a little lonely, I think. The old blue house was made for kids; and now, with everyone grown and gone, it felt so empty.

A church paper fell off the low round coffee table in front of her. She picked it up, put it back, and it fell off again.

This time, when she picked it up, a little ad at the bottom caught her eye. It was two columns wide and about an inch high, with a blue border, and read, "You, Too, Can Be a Missionary." That's how it all began. She called her priest, was in the church office within the hour, and the course was set.

The phone rang about eleven o'clock one day in early June. She answered, "Hello."

"Mrs. Longford?" The voice sounded Hispanic.

"Yes." She smiled into the phone thinking it was another telemarketer.

"My name is Orlando Addison. I am director of the Holy Spirit Episcopal Bilingual School in Tela, Honduras. I need a second-grade teacher for next year. Do you think you can do it?"

He had used the magic words: *Do you think you can do it?*

"Well, yes. I guess I can."

"Good. Then I can expect you in the middle of August?"

"Fine. Will you send me some instructions?"

"Of course. We'll see you in August."

I was listening to all this. She put the phone down, looked at the envelope where she had written "Tela, Honduras," along with the school, his name, and a phone number. I heard her say, "Oh, dear God, what have I done?" She went to the bookshelf, pulled out the encyclopedia, and looked up Honduras.

A few days later, I heard her talking to Candy and Tom, her daughter and son-in-law. "There's something I need to tell you."

"You've got a boyfriend." Laughter.

"No, I'm leaving. I'm going to Honduras to be a teacher missionary."

My heart sank. What would happen to me? I was put away with her things for just a year, or so I thought. The congregation worked and helped raise money for Louise's ticket, things were packed, her passport sent for, a renter found for the house, and lastly, a call to her son, Lew, in Ohio, and daughters Connie and Cindy, both living in North Dakota.

Finally, in the middle of August, Louise left. She was three weeks short of sixty-two, had never seen an ocean, knew very little Spanish, had never been out of the United States, and was off on the adventure of her life.

She was a little nervous flying over the never-ending water. If she were going to go down, she wanted it to be in mounds of snow. The water scared her; there was so much of it. Land appeared several hours later, green and welcoming. To land, the plane circled so close to the mountain that she felt she could reach out and pick the flowers.

The uniformed gentleman next to her rose to leave. Louise looked at her ticket. "Excuse me," she said, "is this where I get off?"

He looked a little irritated but took her ticket, glanced at it, looked back at her, and asked, "What are you doing here?"

"I'm a teaching missionary at a school in Tela."

"Oh," he growled, "one of those." Then his mood seemed to improve. "You don't leave the plane here. This is Tegucigalpa. You sit right there for about thirty more minutes of flying. The plane will land at San Pedro Sula. That is where you get off."

He took a step to leave, stopped, turned, and handed her a card. "If you have any problems, give me a call."

Louise looked at the card—liaison officer between the Honduran Air Force and the US Air Force. A silent "thank you, God" wafted upward.

She had dressed quite appropriately for her trip: a two-piece polyester dress, slip, nylons, all sweat-producing fabrics. Customs was in a metal Quonset hut. The heat was intolerable. Fans helped, but not much.

After emerging to a sea of brownish faces, she located someone she thought must be the school custodian standing at the back, with a sign that read, "Louse Longford." She smiled to herself, thinking *That's got to be me.*

The man was the school's director, Mr. Addison; and as they got into the old cab, with its cracked windows and wires hanging out of the dashboard, she was put in the backseat. She was tall. It was small.

A hole in the seat had been stuffed with filling. Skirting it, she sat like a folded-up gazelle while the two men carried on an animated conversation in front. The intense, sticky heat was alleviated somewhat by the breeze from the driver's open window.

Mr. Addison would stop talking long enough to turn and direct her attention to the banana plantations, the long white plastic bags covering the fruit, and the big Dole and Chiquita trucks pulling in and out of the fields. On the other side of the road spread miles of tall, dense sugarcane fields; and farther, African palm groves covered at least twenty square miles.

Mr. Addison explained, "African palms have no coconuts. Instead, they produce a huge cluster of oil pods, resembling grapes, only much larger. This is a major Honduran business, centered in the little village of San Alejo, where the oil is processed and shipped."

Driving in Honduras is full-time defensive driving, dodging other passing or stopped vehicles, animals, people walking, or bicycles. They all smile and wave as you go by—a friendly people. She found them to be even-tempered, patient, slow, and deliberate, *until* they got behind the wheel of a car.

There was no highway patrol. If an accident happened, someone would go to the nearest station and get a *transito*, the officers who controlled the highway system.

Tropical rains are wonderful. They come and go quickly and are warm and refreshing. Louise's first rain came as she was headed for Tela in the taxi. The rainstorm swept in, and the driver, without ever breaking pace in his conversation with Mr. Addison, reached out the window and moved the broken wiper back and forth manually.

Going into Tela, Louise recognized the picture on the postcard Mr. Addison had sent her. They stopped at a little restaurant where he ordered her a cool drink—a *tamarindo*, the color of a root beer but fruity and not too sweet. This stop was twofold: to acquaint Louise with the main street and to acquaint people with his new teacher from the United States. Because of her height, clothes, and manner, she was easily recognized.

The taxi then took her to the little cement apartment of the Spanish teacher, Miriam, and her daughter, Johanna Luisa. The school's teacherage was full, so Miriam offered a room until Louise found quarters. Miriam spoke no English, and Louise's Spanish was very poor. She was shown her room. It was very small, with a cot and a nail in the wall for clothes.

Because of the extreme heat, she opened her suitcase to air her clothes. They were damp from the humidity, and as she put her white cotton dress on the only nail, she noticed spots of mold already beginning to appear. She frantically began laying out her clothes on the bed. Miriam suggested she put them back in the closed case as soon as they dried. *That's odd,* Louise thought.

At bedtime, she rested uneasily in this strange place; it was so hot and humid she had thrown off the sheet. She woke with a start as something hit her face. She heard buzzing in the air; something flew into her stomach. Another buzz and something hit her thigh and then her leg. She screamed. Miriam came running. *"Es cucarachas,* Louisà" she calmly explained. Louise remembered how everything in the very clean kitchen was covered with a white towel. She had never been around cockroaches before. *Dear God, they were big and ugly.* She cringed and pulled the sheet up over her head.

Several days later, teacher friends found her a room close to the school. It boasted screens on the windows and looked quite secure. Though she left Miriam's home, the two were close friends until she left years later. Little Johanna changed her name and insisted on being called Luisa, like her godmother Louise.

There were many times those first days that she would have loved to have had a camera, such as the afternoon she was going home from school and got caught in another sudden rain. She dashed under an almond tree, which grew like a huge umbrella. A little burro, tied to the trunk, silently ignored her. There the two waited out the storm.

The sky cleared, and she started through town. After the main four or five blocks, she had to pass in front of the noisy cantinas and the old, weathered, unpainted red-light houses. A few inviting women were smiling down from the dilapidated porches.

The rain began again. She stopped under a small overhanging sign, El Chavo, and leaned back against the cement building. Seconds later, a hand holding a bottle of ice-cold Coca-Cola appeared from the doorway, only the wrist and hand visible. She smiled and took it. The hand and forearm appeared again, holding a plastic chair. She laughed, took it, and sat down.

The rain ended, and her drink was finished. She put her head in, said *"gracias,"* and asked what she owed. *"Nada,* Teacher." They smiled, and she went on her way. It was good to know she had someone friendly as an ally, protection if she needed it. *They know who I am*, she thought.

They not only knew who she was, every taxi driver in town knew her name, where she lived, worked, and all the particulars. That was their business. Communication in the third world may be primitive, but it is extremely thorough.

There were guns on the streets. They were on every corner and in front of all the banks, but they didn't bother her as much as the machetes. Those long, sharp knives sent shivers down her spine. The edge was like a razor and always sharpened only one way on the file, which was carried in the back pocket of the jeans. Usually wrapped in newspaper to protect the blade, they were used for everything from clearing paths to protection. It was a way of life for the *campasinos*[4] and those who lived in and around the cities, mountains, farms, and jungles.

Every home had at least one machete, and every person knew how to use it. It took a strong arm to wield one, and Hondurans were built strong across the shoulders. Their upper arms were somewhat shorter, giving them that extra power.

Everything was carried on their backs, loads she didn't think possible. It didn't seem to bother them. Women and children carried firewood in a sling across the back, up, and around the forehead. Backs were strong and patience long.

---

4   peasant, farmer, worker

Louise's first Sunday in Tela was memorable. She had been feeling nauseous and was dehydrated. It was a very hot morning, and as she was about to enter the church, she fainted. She felt strong arms gently lift and support her. Hands soothed her cold, wet skin. Voices were saying, "We are here." She woke up to see four of the blackest women imaginable looking down into her face: Edna, Carol, Clarinda, and Marianne. Louise came from Montana and was not accustomed to being with blacks. Her surprise was noted.

They smiled, patted her arms, and took her to her room at Doña Lela's house, where the doña made her a cup of canella tea. It settled. After two cups, she finally relaxed and slept. Her new friends checked on her many times that day, and until she left years later, they were there for her every minute. They laughed with her in the good times and comforted her in the bad, all except Clarinda.

That tall, outspoken, wonderful woman died, but not before she called Louise to her deathbed, held her hand, and whispered, "You'll never leave Tela, Miss. You are part of us. I can feel the spirits. You will stay."

Those first days in Honduras were made easier by three fellow stateside teachers: Jenny, Dotty, and Benny.

Benny was Costa Rican and a crackerjack of a math teacher. He was one of the very best, his students taking awards in all the competitions, year after year.

He found Louise sitting on the beach several days after she first arrived, looking out over the water, wondering what she was doing there.

"Don't let me frighten you, Louisa. I'm Benny, remember? I think you are homesick."

She was.

"I know what we'll do. Come." He took her to Telamar, the big resort hotel, where they sat, talked, and had a Coca-Cola from the old green-glass bottles. He was quiet, concerned, and knew well the tropics with its beastly heat. Everything seemed better after that.

Hondurans are a formal people. Louise was never called by her given name but always respectfully addressed as *Miss, Teacher, Profa*, or *Mrs. Langford*. Only her closest friends or countrymen called her the Spanish name for Louise: *Louisa*. Many used the English pronunciation with the accent on the *i*; others, the true Spanish form with the accent on the *a*. To the students she was *Miss, Teacher*, or *Mrs. Langford*; and to the *taxistas*, people of the city, and everyone else, she was *Miss, Teacher*, or *Profa*.

Her life changed. She washed on the board and learned it wasn't as simple as it looked. She marveled at the gorgeous flowers and, that first year, suffered in the heat. Slowly, the easy pace won her over. She also learned to endure the cold showers at Doña Lela's. The doña said heating the showers cost too much, so at five in the morning, she stepped into the shower stall and washed her hair in cold, cold water. That took courage. Even in the tropics, it chilled off before the sun came up.

Sunrise was about five thirty, and sunset, around six thirty. It never varied more than a half hour because of their proximity to the equator. There were neither sunrises nor sunsets, so to speak. Morning would come with a blast of light, and with it the intense heat, rapidly turning all the nightly dew into humidity. There was no dusk, as she knew it. Night would literally fall, so quickly she could hardly catch a photo of that huge orange ball disappearing into the sea.

Tela was initially built on the coast by the United Fruit Company before the company moved inland. The main hotels and restaurants faced the ocean on the beachfront, where she often spent her evenings enjoying camaraderie with travelers, other teachers, and friends.

Palms lined the coast and spread inland well into the mountains. They were beautiful, tall, graceful, the huge long fronds flexing their leafy fingers as they caught the gentle breezes. The palms on the beaches were the tall coconut palms arching up from bulbs that stood nearly four feet tall, their sturdy trunks often bent from the ocean winds, and produced clusters of green or yellow coconuts.

Stately royal palms, their smooth white trunks reaching high in the air, often lined parkways and resort avenues, while the graceful princess palms, with four or more trunks coming from a single bulb, were usually found in the gardens and lawns of homes.

African palms and their oil-producing pods were the commercial palms. Workers used caution as their fruit drew snakes, tarantulas, and insects. The woody trunks housed many forms of ferns and philodendrons and were breathtaking to see. There were many other palms native to these tropics. Louise found it so restful to watch as the graceful fronds moved to and fro in the soft breezes.

In the beginning, there were no televisions and few radios, newspapers, and telephones. The power ran six hours on and six hours off. The country was emerging from a military government to a more democratic form. Change was hard. The military controlled the electrical power; and the government, the telephone. When disputes arose between the two factions, one utility would be shut off, with the other retaliating likewise. People just shook their heads, smiled, and learned to live with it.

There was no air-conditioning in the schools those first years, and only two or three little fans operated per room. The heat was overwhelming. School was from 7:00 a.m. to 2:00 p.m., with twenty minutes for lunch and twenty minutes for recess.

Her teaching supplies consisted of a notebook, ruler, pen, and whiteout. There was a large blackboard, and she was given three pieces of chalk to last a week. Books were all in English—older ones sent from the States and were often moldy and musty from the tropical humidity.

She never used Spanish in her classes. From the very beginning, every word she taught was in English. She looked at those little faces, knowing they did not understand. She spoke slowly and clearly, over and over, using pictures and repetition. They learned, oh, how they learned— their minds, like little sponges, absorbing each word.

On the twenty-second of April, as she stood in front of her class in this other part of the world, she suddenly, for no apparent reason, felt a few soft tears running down her cheeks. She looked at her watch. It was 7:15 a.m., the exact time Lennie had stopped breathing two years before. It seemed to be God's gentle way of saying "I am here, Louise."

CHAPTER 2

To be a teacher in Honduras was a profession equal to, and demanding the same respect as, that of a doctor or lawyer. And as in anything, they come good, bad, uncaring, and dedicated.

Benny was one of those special educators; he cared. Several weeks into the school year, he noticed Louise was flushed.

"What's the matter, Louisa?"

"I feel horrible. I am so tired, my knees hurt, and my feet hurt. I hurt all over."

"Louisa, I'm taking you to the doctor right now," he said. "Would you mind if I took you to a doctor I know?"

"No, of course not."

They left immediately.

Doctor visits were not the same as in the States. There were no appointments. Louise paid the set fee when she checked in. If it came to more, the doctor would collect the balance at the end of her exam. She took a seat and waited her turn. When her name was called, Benny stood and smiled. "I'm going in with you. He doesn't speak English. Don't worry. I'll turn my head."

Dr. Rivas shook her hand; he was very friendly and very handsome. The men talked, and Benny translated her symptoms. Dr. Rivas asked her age. She told him, "Sixty-two."

"Are you sure?" he asked.

"Yes."

He thought for a while. "Mrs. Langford, what all do you do for a day?"

She didn't answer, just looked at Benny.

Dr. Rivas looked at Benny and shook his head, saying, "I observed your ankles."

These Latins, Louise thought.

The doctor continued, "And I think you are lacking oxygen in your blood. A person your age needs much oxygen, and possibly you have arthritis bothering you."

From the frown on her face, he knew he had made a mistake. Deciding he needed some tests run, he ordered her to the lab. She went, secretly worried they might use an old needle.

Though the walls weren't painted, everything seemed sterile. They did use a new needle, even rubber gloves, and the blood drawing was excellently done. She had to pay promptly for the lab work; the total was 225L ($22.25). Results were ready in one hour, sealed in an envelope, and delivered to Louise to give to the doctor.

Returning to his office, she was immediately taken in. Dr. Rivas was happy, gave her lab tests back to her, and said, "Mrs. Langford, you have contracted a virus that you probably would not notice in Montana, but here in the tropics, it could be very bad. I will give you a prescription, and you will feel better soon. Also"—he hesitated then charged ahead—"you are simply beginning to wear out and should not be doing so much."

He handed her the prescription, and she left for the pharmacy. Her prescription was returned to her with her medicine.

Two days later, her lips were swollen and split. Benny immediately rushed her back to the doctor. He became noticeably upset when he saw her and called in another physician. They decided she needed an injection. She took the prescription to the pharmacy, bought the syringe and medicine, and took it back to the doctor. Since he had no office nurse, he gave her the shot. Benny stood by.

The doctor came to the school every day to check on her and also kept track of her through some of her friends who happened to live next door to him.

After his last checkup, he reminded her, "You have my son next year, and I must keep you in good health as you are a good teacher and a nice person, and my family is very interested in you. We want you well." She later learned that the parents of three of her own students were doctors, news which greatly reassured her family back in the States.

The following week, Benny told her, "Saturday I will take you to the market to acquaint you with our foods."

They were at the *mercado* early, before the oppressive heat. While learning what was in some of the various big hundred-pound sacks, which contained everything from rice to dog food and peanuts to poultry, he introduced her to one of his friends. "Louisa, I want you to meet Juan."

Juan was young, thin, and obviously poor but clean. He was looking at pencils and small notebooks. "I'd like to tell you about Juan," Benny continued.

"He teaches high up in the mountains above Rio Leòn. After leaving the bus, he hikes ten kilometers up the mountain to his school. He sleeps on the ground. The children have few clothes, no shoes, and come to school when they can. School is a one-sided lean-to. They sit on the ground or a tree stump.

"Every Friday, each child brings an egg to school. Saturday, he carefully packs the eggs and walks back down the mountain. He brings them here and sells them for money to buy pencils and paper for his students to use the following week."

Juan smiled at Louise and reached out to shake her hand, which is done in Honduras by a slight sliding down of the fingers. They never clasp or grip a hand.

She asked Benny to tell Juan she was truly proud to meet him and would like to help him, if that was all right. He held the one-hundred-lempira bill she handed him and nodded to her. His eyes said "thank you."

"How many years have you, Miss?" her students would ask. She just smiled. One of the best-kept secrets at school was Louise's age. Honduran women her age were considered old. She intended to keep them guessing as long as she could. She tried to always look her best, but it was difficult to learn the ins and outs of salons in a different culture.

Hondurans are very conscientious about their appearance. No matter how poor, they are groomed and clean. Her Lewistown friend, Coty Zahler, who had taught her enough basic Spanish to help her get by, had stressed how women in Central America were especially attentive to their hair and their shoes. Teachers in all the schools were immaculately dressed, uniforms always clean and pressed.

Manicures and pedicures were common among most professional men and women. Louise finally took the big step and had a pedicure. Her feet were soaked, massaged, the skin exfoliated, nails trimmed, polished, and even decorated—all for a pittance. It felt wonderful.

Haircuts, on the other hand, were a problem. She had a hard time trying to explain what she wanted. No matter what Louise tried to tell her,

Rosie would cut it like she thought it should be; and if it was too short, she would just shrug. Louise tried another beautician.

Her last appointment was the day the stylist's husband was brought into the salon by the police. The woman was crying, yelling at her husband, screaming at the police, and cutting Louise's hair—all at the same time. Louise saw her hair falling to the floor, threw her hands over her head and yelled, "No!"

Her neighbors taught her to use the word *trim* in Spanish and introduced her to an older woman who traveled house to house with her scissors. Louise was relieved. She wore her hair in an easy bob, which turned under in the high humidity just as she wanted, and colored it a nice, soft brown, something she had done for years.

On a Monday morning, during reading class, Harry raised his hand. He was tall, easygoing, black, always happy, had a big smile, and spoke exceptionally good English.

"Yes, Harry?"

"You've painted your hair, Miss."

"I've what?" she asked.

"You've painted your hair," he said, and the whole class laughed.

They loved to catch her on little cultural things and tried to outdo each other with horrible snake stories to scare her or see her shudder. She always laughed with them; she knew they loved her. Years later, on September 11, Harry's aunt would be one of the many killed when the twin towers came down in New York City.

Life in Central America cannot be complete without soccer—an absolute in any Honduran boy's life. It's in their blood, and their national sport. Students may not know the names of their government leaders, but they know every player on the national team and all their statistics. From the time they take their first step, they kick a ball, bottle cap, can, something.

Louise knew absolutely nothing about the game, but the boys knew everything, so after school she walked her little second graders to the big soccer stadium in the city to practice and play. Sometimes, the street boys would challenge them to a game, playing without shoes, using the conch shell as the official whistle, and always winning by a huge margin.

Eventually, Angel, Giancarlo's father, began to show up and help organize the team. It grew; third graders wanted to be included and also the fourth-grade boys. Every night, after school, Louise herded her growing group of boys to the stadium.

The school finally stepped in and said she would have to stop. She certainly understood, but students were enraged. Parents came to school to protest, and finally, an after-school soccer program was implemented. She was relieved. She probably knew less about the game than any of the boys, but she talked as though she did; it was something she learned from them.

Hand in hand with their love of soccer came their dedication to country. The show of flags pulled them together. It began early in the fall. Blue-and-white-striped flags popped up in business windows, schools, and homes. Only during the month of September was the Honduran flag flown.

September 15 was Independence Day. All schools in the Tela area had to march in the big parade. This meant all classes, kinder up through eleventh. They practiced for weeks, tying up highways and any level field. There were close to thirty schools in the area, both government and private—some with only a few students, some with hundreds. Only private schools were bilingual.

Beginning in the morning heat at seven, it ended after eleven; bodies drenched with sweat and weak from the sun. Bands played, baton twirlers strutted, and honor students led their classes, pride in their country shining from all their faces.

School after school paraded down the long, hot road through town, each in their school's uniform, mandatory in Honduras. Mothers and teachers ran alongside the marchers, giving water and oranges to the students when they slowed or stopped for presentations in front of the dignitaries. Louise dreaded that long, hot walk on those uneven streets, especially with her leg. She'd had extensive surgery on her left knee, and it was still weak. But she did it, every year.

On those warm evenings, after a long, hot day at school, Louise would sit and relax with friends at the Casa Azul, a little restaurant owned by Canadians, Claude and Francine. She knew the unwritten rules: never walk on the beach at night, and be off the streets and home before dark. Staying a bit too late one night, she began walking.

The streets were totally deserted. Tall, old wooden buildings, with their boarded-up windows, cast eerie shadows in front and in back of her. The old-fashioned black lamps at the beginning and end of the street gave off little light. Her footsteps echoed in the silence.

She was walking as fast as she could in the middle of the street, becoming more frightened with every step. Almost to the end, where it branched into the road across the bridge, she heard a soft voice, clear as a bell, from behind the board fence to her right. "It's all right, Teacher. We know you are there."

Relief washed over her. She calmed and made it across the bridge and down the path to the house. It was the same bridge where she would be robbed at gunpoint a few days later.

She had gone to the city with Gerard, the fifth-grade teacher. On the way home, they were talking. A man suddenly appeared in front of them, waving a pistol and shouting "*dinero!*" His hand was shaking;

that bothered Louise. She tossed fifty lempiras at the ground in front of him and started to walk away.

"Louise," Gerard shouted. "Stop! Be careful!"

She kept on walking. As far as she was concerned, it was over. She had thrown caution to the wind, a bit too sure of herself. Within the next few hours, the robber killed a man on the same bridge, just a few feet before the school. She realized how foolish she had been and again reminded herself where she was. *Third world, Louise, third world.*

There were few modern conveniences. Her wash was done on the washboard out on Doña Lela's wooden back porch. Both Lupè and Lela would smile and say, "Make it sing, Miss." Struggling with her wash on a Saturday morning, she was bent over the sink, her feet next to the base opening underneath. Something bit the end of her toe, hard.

"Oh, dear God!" she screamed. "I've been bitten by a snake." Near hysterics, she was sure she was going to die.

Doña Lela came running, yelling for Doña Aurora next door. Suddenly, Lela stopped, a smile spreading across her face. "*Es Tino,*" she said, and stooped to put her fingers down for her pet parrot.

Tino was slowly waddling from under the sink, across to Doña Lela, wanting up on her shoulder while cocking her head and giving Louise the evil eye. A tissue stopped the droplets of blood from Tino's warning bite on her big toe, and knowing there was no snake brought on a smile.

"Come, Louisa, have *cafè,*" said Lela.

Doña Aurora left and reappeared as they were drinking their coffee. Her arms were held high, each hand grasping the tail of a four-foot-long iguana, its feet tied behind. The women were thrilled.

"I will cook," announced Lela.

Louise swallowed. Killing iguanas was supposed to be illegal, but no one paid attention to the law. Boys would catch and sell them. It was considered a delicacy.

She knew what was coming. Two short hours later, there was a knock on her door. The plate, proudly held by Doña Lela, was thrust at her. The meat was circular, white, and covered with a light creamy sauce. She couldn't refuse it, but her stomach was already sending negative signals. She took a bite to please Doña Lela; thanked her, saying how delicious it was; and the minute the door shut, ran for the bathroom.

There were rats. She wasn't used to rats in Montana. "*Ratòns*," Doña Lela called them, and this short, stocky woman sat in the kitchen at night, perched up on a stool, her hand clamped around the handle of her machete, waiting. In the dark hours of early morning, Louise heard the machete hit against wood and tile, along with a few unintelligible Spanish phrases.

"Did you get the *ratòn?*" Louise asked the next day.

"*Sí*," Doña Lela answered, "and tonight I will get the other."

Fear of the unknown can create monsters. One quiet evening, Doña Lela was having church. From her window, Louise watched the serious faces of five or six arrivals, an uneasy feeling stealing through her. She was becoming cautious of many things.

A short time later, she heard "North American," then low voices fluctuating up and down, some almost sharp. She became alarmed. What a fool she had been, trusting so completely. She waited for her chance, quietly sneaked out of her room, made a dash for the gate, and ran the eight blocks to the Episcopal House where the other teachers lived.

As she bolted in the front door, she said breathlessly, "Something is going on." She finished with "I'm scared." Benny and several other friends sat and talked with her, finally walking her back through the night to her room.

Doña Lela met them at the gate. "What happened, Louisa? Why did you leave so quickly? We were going to ask you to join us. It was a good meeting. Some of us spoke in tongues."

Realizing what she had heard, Louise finally relaxed. Sleep came much, much later.

Doña Lela professed an Evangelical faith; however, old habits never seem to go away. She had to leave town for a few days. Louise would be alone. Stopping by to pick her up for school one morning during Lela's absence, Benny grinned as she came out.

"What's up, Benny?"

He pointed. Above her door was a pair of scissors, hanging point down.

"A little bit of voodoo," he said, still smiling. "She's protecting you."

Louise's room at Doña Lela's sat a little lower than ground level. It was nice, fresh, and cool, with the exception of the urine smell that blew through whenever Lela's dog went outside. Quietly, she began looking for another apartment.

There was much to learn. Cultures seemed simple but so different. She tried to learn patience, to let them show her their ways. They had so much to give, but they wouldn't push it on to anyone. They had learned to exist truly, day to day.

The tiniest thing could cause big problems. The only warning Louise had when she left the States was *don't ever pick up a child you don't know*. She made that mistake once on a bus. Human trafficking had alerted every parent. They were especially cautious of North Americans, some of whom had been arrested smuggling children out of the country.

En route to San Pedro Sula on an early morning bus, she noticed a young mother standing, holding a new baby. Her little girl was trying to hold on to the mother's skirt. Louise reached out, picked up the little girl, and set her on her lap. Talking on the bus stopped. Silence. All eyes were on Louise.

What have I done? she thought. Then she remembered, smiled, set the baby girl back on the floor, got up, and gave the mother the seat.

About a block from El Chavo was a tiny open restaurant called the Chavalita. It sat in the central bus terminal. Louise often liked to stop and get a *tajada*, mainly to people-watch.

Marta put in fried plantains,[5] added shredded cabbage covered with some juicy gravy, a piece of chicken, more *plantains*, more cabbage topped off with chicken gizzards, chicken feet, and more gravy. Only, when Louise ordered it, there were no gizzards or feet, just a nice piece of white meat.

The street boys would see her coming and run for the Chavalita. They were always hungry and knew she'd buy a couple of *tajadas* they could share.

Sometimes she would see a family sitting at a table waiting for a bus to the mountains, the *niños* obviously hungry. Taking her *tajada* back to the kitchen, she would have them put some chicken feet on top, then take it over to the table and tell them, "I am sorry, but I am late for school and have no time to eat. Would you permit me to give this to the *niños, por favor?*" They would wait a moment, smile, and nod. As she left through the back door, Marta would wink and hand her a sack filled with some fried *plantains* and a piece of chicken.

Teacher worked hard at learning more Spanish, but her English kept getting in the way, and there was so much else to do. She got along fine. She found a smile, and her limited, animated vocabulary got her through.

---

5   also called *platenos*, large green bananas

Certainly, there were problems. When she first arrived in Tela, the taxistas asked where her husband was. She thought she was telling them he was dead.[6] Instead, she had advised them he was scared,[7] never noticing their slight smile.

Most evenings during the first eight or nine years meant a trip to the Casa Azul to meet friends, speak some English, and have a snack or a drink. She was safe there and could relax.

She decided the language was pretty simple and tried using some new word endings. Sitting with a large group of friends one evening, she told them she was *embarazado*, assuming she was saying she was embarrassed.

They looked at her with astonishment. "Are you sure, Louise?"

She answered, "Of course, I was *so* embarrassed."

The laughter was hilarious.

"Do you know what you said?" Veronique asked.

She frowned.

Francine said, "You just announced you were pregnant."

"Oh no!" Hoots and howls shamed her into more lessons.

Sitting at the little restaurant, she enjoyed watching the people pass by, usually on bicycles. It was unbelievable how many different ways there were to carry someone on a bicycle.

Young prostitutes sauntered by, often a novice with them. They taught the new girl how to walk, smile, and approach men. Louise knew most of the women and always acknowledged them. She had gone to their

---

[6]   *muerto*

[7]   *miedo*

house of business and helped two of their children get treatment in the medical brigades.

Prostitution is a way of life in the third world. Some survive to have normal lives; most don't. Human trafficking is a huge problem in Honduras. San Pedro Sula had a reputation for being one of the worst. Drug-induced prostitutes filled the cribs and stables (small sectioned houses of prostitution) for streets on end. Life was hard. After a short time, they eventually became sick—usually with AIDS—and died. Most never reached twenty-five. Louise shivered when she saw young girls, barely sixteen, walking the streets, luring men into conversations; many of these men expatriates from North America.

Abuse began young. Often, girls were kidnapped and sold into prostitution; others simply had no other place to go. An institution called the School of the Little Rosas was begun by the Episcopal Church in San Pedro Sula—a home for exploited and abused girls, where they were taught and trained for a new life.

She moved from Doña Lela's to a cabaña on the ocean. Walking past the big hotel compound on her way home one evening, someone grabbed her wrist from behind.

A *muchacho*[8] tried to force her little purse from her hand by biting through her wrist. His friend held the machete and the bike which had carried them silently up behind her. She didn't let go. Her keys were in the bag.

A pickup loaded with young blacks drove by, saw what was happening, and two or three men jumped out to help her. The two boys threw her in the watery street and ran for their lives.

"Teacher, we know who you are," said the driver in perfect English as he helped her stand. "You teach with my cousin, Alibel. I will help you.

---

[8]   young man

Where can I take you?" They left her at the Casa Azul, and bedraggled, wet Louise received the tender loving care she needed.

The next morning, she left the house for school. Her two wrists were bandaged—one from being bitten, and the other sprained from hitting the street. As she was walking her bike down the hill and through the town, people came out of their homes, apartments, businesses, and cantinas, crowding around her.

"Teacher, we are so sorry. We are not like that." They took her bike, her book bag, supported her arms, and walked her to the school gate. Some of the mothers put extra food in their children's lunches to fatten her up. They said she was too skinny.

Walking to school just after sunup was refreshing and was one of her favorite times of the day—watching the city wake up. Sometimes she would see a few street people bathing in the pools of water left standing from the night's rain. She learned to walk through many different situations without ever showing surprise. She just tucked them away in her mind, to tell her grandchildren.

A road had been cleared between the homes on the east side and the city. There was only one obstacle: a huge round boulder, at least seven feet in height. It sat right in the center of the road. Early in the morning, on her way to school, Louise noticed a little man sitting on top of the monstrous rock. He was an older man, and in his hand he held a brick hammer and a chisel.

She stopped, grinned at him, and shook her head. He read her mind, gave her a toothless smile, and nodded. She laughed and went on. *Ridiculous,* she thought. She knew Hondurans didn't have heavy work equipment. Here, everything was done by hand. But this? *No.*

He worked every day, tapping away at the big rock; and every morning, she would stop and smile. He would grin and say, "*Buenas dias,* señora."

Sometimes, in the afternoon, she would stop at the *pulperìa* there by the side of the road and pay the owner to give the little chiseler a coke.

One morning, he waved at her and pointed. A large chunk was missing, although very little compared to the size of the rock. She arranged with the *pulperìa* owner to see that he had a soft drink every day. He would watch for her and always greet her as she went by, headed back home from school. Gradually, week after week, as the hot sun beat down, the pile of little chunks grew larger.

Then, three months after he began, the final pieces began to crumble. There was a little celebration by the three of them—the storeowner, the little chiseler, and Louise. She shook his hand and congratulated him, even bought him a beer.

Louise bought a used Ford Ranger pickup with a topper and had benches built in the back. It opened up a new world. The pickup was wonderful, but getting her license was totally frustrating. The exam was in Spanish. When she asked if they had an English version, they simply changed each word from Spanish to English, which left sentences that made no sense. The questions were unlike anything she had ever thought of. She tried, barely making 70 percent. They frowned but finally gave her the license.

It occurred to her a little gratuity might have helped, especially when she saw a lovely young Englishwoman being helped with her exam by an amorous officer. She laughed to herself; she couldn't compete with the looks, but she could have tried the money.

One of the problems with the government's school and hospital programs was that the government often failed to pay their teachers and nurses for several months. When the situation became intolerable, the teachers and nurses called in the taxistas.

The country would be thrown into lockdown with roadblocks. It was so well organized that nothing moved—not ambulances, produce trucks, absolutely nothing—until the president agreed to their demands, called out the riot squads, and opened the roads. To be caught in one of these roadblocks was frightening, rendering a person totally helpless. It gave thought to the power of the common people: strong, swift, and sure.

After her first rainy encounter in front of the little cantina, El Chavo, she met Vilma who tended bar there. She lived in the hills and caught the bus to work each day. Her daughter had vamoosed and left Vilma to raise the grandchildren.

Christmas in this country was a time when families got together, ate tamales, lit firecrackers, and enjoyed each other. On Christmas Eve, they dressed in their best and went to church or walked in Central Park. As Louise passed the cantina on her way to church on Christmas Eve, Vilma said, "Be sure to stop and see my *nietas*[9] on your way home."

"Of course," Louise said, wondering how this would work with a cantina full of happy drunks.

She saw the two girls—each dressed in their best, one in pink and one in soft green—sitting in front of the cantina. People stopped and talked to them, and Vilma glowed with pride. Anticipating just such an occasion, Louise had two dolls gift-wrapped and ready. They carefully opened the presents, shouting with glee. *The thought crossed Louise's mind that they had never had a gift.*

The next morning, as she was on her way to church, Vilma stepped out of the cantina and stopped her. "Teacher," she said softly, "this is all I have, and I want you to have it."

She pressed a small, thin gold ring into Louise's hand. Louise started to object, quickly saw her error, and thanked Vilma. Turning down a gift was not done. She wore the ring until it wouldn't keep its shape.

---

[9]   granddaughters

Visiting Vilma's home in the mountains was much like entering another world. In these areas, water was carried and the wash was usually done in streams, using rocks for scrub boards. Louise was always asked inside her home for café. Vilma had a special cup without a handle, and it was cracked, but when Louise came to visit, she drank coffee from that cup. She saw the dirt floor, the grime, shut her eyes, and drank.

Word reached Louise that Vilma's five-year-old grandson was badly burned by a candle-caused fire in the bedding. He slept on the rocks and cool dirt floor to keep the pain and fever down. Louise took salves and dressings and drove the five miles to Vilma's. Blisters on his face and neck had begun to heal. Grandmother Vilma had tended to him well. He healed but, sadly, was left with a bad eye.

At Christmas, Louise took Vilma a large sack full of food and gifts for the three children. The boy was sitting by the road and, as Louise drove up, excitedly called his grandmother. Vilma greeted her. "He has been watching for you for two days. He told me he knew you would come."

Chapter 3

A major problem for Louise and other volunteers was visas. Every three months, they had to be renewed, which meant leaving the country for three days in order to get their passports stamped, both when leaving and entering. It was a long, uncomfortable trip on the autobus.

Louise was a people-watcher and enjoyed the country folk and their interaction on the slow chicken buses. One old grandma sitting next to her took out an ear of corn, ate a row, and handed it to Louise, indicating she could have a row or two. Louise smiled, declined, and the old lady stuck it back into her pocket for later.

Vendors, with their baskets of hot food, hopped on the bus at every stop. The pie-looking tortilla with a bump on top intrigued her. She bought one, full of delicious meat, onions, chilies, and a whole boiled egg, all sealed in a corn tortilla and fried.

She took the trip to Copan with a friend named Paul. Both needed to exit the country to renew their visas. Situated next to the Guatemalan border, Copan Ruinas was a perfect trip. The bus took them past the valleys of tobacco fields and the little smokehouses, where the tobacco leaves were processed, and on into Copan.

They arrived on Christmas Eve and decided to join the quiet little families, both Honduran and Guatemalan, waiting outside the old church. When the doors were opened, they entered, careful to sit on the side that had a roof; a good portion of it had disappeared. The starry night lent its own aura to the simple service done in the native tongue. Afterward, they joined the many in the large central park in front of the church. It was *Navidad*[10] and everyone visited in the park. Louise noticed all the men had new brown work shoes, a gift from the employers in the tobacco fields.

Just after dawn the next day, they toured the ruins, which were especially wondrous in the early morning with the dew-laden grass and mossy steps. Then it was time to continue their journey. She and Paul had been instructed to wait for their Guatemalan ride on a little bridge. When an old pickup came by with a fellow leaning out shouting "*Frontera,*"[11] they climbed on.

The mountains of Guatemala are much like Montana, and she concentrated on them. She was scared to death. There were eighteen people crammed into the pickup. She was lucky enough to be in front.

The driver was not a good one, and he was going too fast over the narrow winding mountainous road. Often, she could see over the side; it was a long way down. At one point, the driver was looking out his window toward the back. She saw the edge come up and yelled. He swung back onto the road, explaining, defensively, that his back tire was low.

They made it to the border. The barbed wire fence stretched for miles. Soldiers were stationed at intervals and around the entrance to the migration office. They asked for her passport, looked at her, and stamped it. She paid the fee for leaving the country and was escorted outside.

Silently, she began the hundred-yard trek across a dry, desolate, quiet no-man's-land to the next barbed wire fence, more soldiers, and Guatemala. Then it was inside another migration office where she was stamped into that country.

---

[10]   Christmas

[11]   border

A bus took them to a small town where they watched a muchacho buy his first machete at an open *tienda*[12] on the street. A purple throw caught Louise's eye, and she bought it for her couch. Afterward, they looked for food and a place to sleep.

Two mornings later, the entire process was reversed, and they were back in Copan to begin the long trip back to Tela. She dreaded the days out. She often thought of bribing officers to stamp her book, but getting caught meant trouble.

Her next three-day trip came with an invitation to accompany another friend, Mike, to Cancún, where he was meeting his son. He knew she had to leave the country and offered to take her with him. They flew to Cancún, found lodging and meals. The following day, they boarded the bus to see the Mayan ruins at Chichen Itza. Mike was an architect, and having him as a guide opened an entirely new understanding of this ancient civilization.

He suggested a trip to Merida, Uxmal, and then to Valladolid, where they stayed, drinking in the history of the monastery and the church with its tall, tall doors. The next day, they caught a bus south to the small town of Muna; its bicycle taxis ferrying passengers up and down the streets.

From there, they hopped yet another bus, bumping along the two-rutted road through the fields of pampas grass—he in the front of the bus, and she toward the back. The grass grew high on both sides of the road; all that was visible for miles.

Suddenly, the bus braked. A pickup had pulled out across the road in front, blocking them totally. Soldiers stepped out and walked up to the bus.

It was quiet. People sat motionless. She saw the young mother next to her slip her ring into the baby's shoe. Louise had hidden most of her money in a decorator pocket near the bottom of her jeans.

---

[12] shop

The bus was full. The officer in charge stomped up the two metal steps and began walking toward the back, looking over each passenger. When he came to Louise, he stopped and looked at her. "*Passaportè,*"[13] he ordered.

She produced it. Law said she didn't have to let it out of her hands, but there was no law here. He took it, looked at it, waited, and handed it back. She was sure every person on the bus could hear her heart pounding.

Her mind was saying: *This was what you read about in the newspapers. Two Americans found dead along the highway, hidden in the tall grass, and no one knew a thing.* She took deep breaths and tried to look calm. She sat, frozen.

The officer turned, slowly walking back to the front, his footsteps audible in the quiet. He turned, looked back again, stepped off, and yelled at the pickup.

It backed into the grass, and the old bus lurched through. Mike looked back at her and smiled. She was the same age as his mother, and he was concerned for her. He suggested they get off when they came to the main road.

Sitting in the hot sun for almost an hour, they waited for a car, a bus—something going north. Louise was trying not to panic. *This was a stupid move,* she thought to herself.

When she had all but given up hope, along came a little Volkswagen full of at least six workers packed into the tiny interior. They stopped, smiling. There were friendly handshakes, and yes, Louise and Mike could squeeze in.

Louise was sure she was heavier than the fellow she was sitting on, but with every mile they traveled north, she was happier.

---

[13] passport

Back at last, they had a quick supper and went out into the streets of Merida to watch the dancers perform. Happy women vendors outfitted her in a native dress, the same as they were wearing. They were little more than half as tall as she. Finished, they stood back and looked at her, clapping their hands, telling her how beautiful she was. After so much enthusiasm, she had to buy it.

The next day, it was back to Cancún, followed by a two-day idyllic stay at Isla Mujeres, and then her return to Tela. She didn't see Mike again. After visiting his son, he left to teach in Korea. But he had propelled her through an experience of a lifetime in a Mexico she could love—a Mexico she would someday like to see again, full of warm, friendly people.

Another quick three-day trip into Guatemala took Louise through the westernmost port of entry. The bus was comfortable, and the new road through the winding rocky mountains reminded her of her home state. She was able to sit back and thoroughly relax.

As they were getting close to Esquipulas, Guatemala, she was looking out her window and saw what resembled a miniature town. It looked almost like it had come from a Disney movie. There were odd-shaped little houses in a myriad of colors: pink, all shades of blues and greens, yellows, reds . . . all different. They were situated in back of a very large church. The bus stopped in the parking area.

On the huge expanse of lawn and cement, in and around the church, she saw people of every walk of life—many people. Most noticeable was the amount of lame, bedridden, and those in wheelchairs. This was the great Esquipulas Basilica, home of the Black Christ, known throughout Central America as a healing shrine.

Entering, she found a service already in progress. There were no chairs. The large crowd all stood, with the exception of those in front who were on stretchers or in wheelchairs. Louise stepped back into the foyer and over to the side, where she could look at the gorgeous tapestries that covered the walls.

She was standing, totally immersed in the fine work of an especially beautiful hanging, when she felt a little hand fit into hers. A small voice said, *"La Paz."*[14] Louise answered the same, smiling, still holding the small hand. Another second, and the little girl skipped off.

Louise later viewed the Black Christ in its glass case at the side of the altar. The whole scene—the church, the crowds, the statue, the tapestries—every different thing was so interesting. But the special moment was feeling that little hand in hers.

Back outside, she saw the little colored houses, the tiny town she had seen from the bus. It was located in back of the church. It was a cemetery. In Guatemala, they care for their own long after death.

To stop the three-day-out trips, Louise finally applied for her Honduran residency. The first lawyer disappeared with her money. The second application took about two years. She was finally told to check with the US Embassy in Tegucigalpa.

The trip to Tegucigalpa from Tela was eight hours on the direct bus. It was horrendous; the road into the city was mountainous, winding, and driven at a speed that sent travelers' stomachs flip-flopping. She was sick when she arrived. She found a room over the local police station and tried to sleep. The US Embassy was across the city from the bus station. She got a taxi and arrived early in the morning. Her return ticket to Tela was for that afternoon.

Lines of people filled the sidewalks circling the embassy, each holding a number—a number which had cost them fifty dollars in hopes of getting their visa to the United States. They were all watching. She felt almost guilty when she pulled out her passport and was permitted inside.

---

14   [14] the peace

The secretary, who was Honduran, could not understand the term *widow*. It seemed to take forever to make the agent understand. She then asked for Louise's social security award sheet for that year.

"It's back in the States," answered Louise.

"I'm sorry, Miss. We will need a copy. Perhaps you can call them and have it sent."

Her mind was racing. There was nothing to do but go out and find a phone. She looked. There were plenty of phones, but none that would connect out of the country. Frantic, as the minutes were flying by, she looked up to the left of the offices. The embassy was a large two-building unit; the offices for visas, passports, etc., were on the right, and the ambassador's office was to the left.

Wondering what to do, she stopped and thought for a few moments, eyeing the actual embassy. Surely, they had a phone she could use to reach the United States. She walked up the cement walk to the door. From out of nowhere, a US marine was facing her, totally blocking the entrance. He smiled and asked how he could help her.

"I need a phone to the US, and there is no time to go back through the city," Louise told him.

"Is this an emergency call?"

"Well, I have to have papers for my residency. My bus leaves for Tela in a few hours. Surely, since this is my embassy, you can help me."

He smiled again. Another marine had appeared. The door opened, and two more marines motioned her in. They were extremely courteous but firm.

"May we have your purse, ma'am?"

She handed it over.

"Please empty your pockets."

She did.

"Your name please."

She gave her name, address, where she worked, all the information she felt they would need. As a badge with a ribbon was put around her neck, a lovely young woman appeared on the stairs in front of her. She spoke perfect English and was most polite.

"Follow me please."

Louise went up the plush carpeted stairway into a very comfortable waiting room.

"Please wait here, Mrs. Langford. All you need is a telephone to the States?"

"Yes, and a fax to receive information, if possible."

The gentleman who stepped into the room from another office was cordial, friendly, and obviously busy; but he gave her his card saying, "Mrs. Langford, I am the assistant to the ambassador. We are happy to help you. My secretary will see that you have whatever you need. I have a meeting, so please excuse me. You have my card. Please feel free to call me if I can ever be of assistance."

To his secretary, he said, "Make sure the door stays closed," and he nodded to his office.

The phone sat on the table. Louise called Tom, her son-in-law, in Lewistown, Montana. The call went right through.

"Tom, I need my yearly award sheet from Social Security. Can you fax it right back? I am at the US Embassy." She gave him the number.

"I'm here alone, but I'll try," he answered.

He didn't hesitate. He left his business, drove to the house, found the paper, and it came through the fax machine in less than a half hour.

"Thank you so much," she said to the secretary.

She was shown out, escorted down the carpeted stairs, relieved of her visitor's neckband, given her purse, and ushered out the door. She had been in the United States Embassy. How exciting!

The paper was delivered to the agent back in the office building. She seemed surprised Louise had been in the embassy and told Louise that things seemed to be in order. Just be patient and wait a few weeks—again.

Her passport tucked securely away in her purse, she left the compound, once more passing through the crowds of waiting hopefuls, each clutching their number. She arrived at the terminal with just enough time to save her seat, and was on the long road back to Tela. It would be close to midnight when she arrived, but what a day!

Back in Tela, she waited. Weeks went by, and she began haunting the migration office. They just smiled and said, "Nothing, Miss."

"What's wrong, Alan?" she asked her young lawyer. "They don't seem to be doing anything. It's been months."

"Mrs. Langford," he answered, "do you remember when the transitos stopped you twice a day, checking your license, registration, and papers? You finally gave the sergeant some money, and the problem went away. You do remember?"

It was a sore subject. She was still angry about it but said, "Yes, Alan."

"Well, it's that way, Miss. If you really want your residency, go see them and slip them some money."

"No," she said.

"Okay," he said and shrugged.

Monday morning, she left school and went to the migration office.

"Good morning, Miss," Carlita said. "I'm sorry, no news today."

Louise swallowed and slid two five-hundred-lempira bills across the table. "I know how hard you've worked on this, and I want you to know I appreciate all your help."

Carlita jumped up. "One moment, Miss." She ran quickly to the little office of her boss, the migration officer, obviously handing him one of the bills. They both came back—he, with a fingerprinting kit, and she, with forms that were quickly rolled into the old, worn-out Royal typewriter. She began, "Mother's name, maiden name, date of birth, place of birth . . ."

There was no water, so after they finished, she used a tissue to wipe off what fingerprinting ink she could. Saying it would be one to two days, the officer walked her out and down the stairs. At the bottom, he said, "A bottle of good tequila would be a nice gift for the secretary of migration in Tegucigalpa."

She was back in the hour with the bottle, gift-wrapped. He nodded. "This will do."

That evening, her friend Carol said, "That is how my people are, but I am not proud of it."

Four days later, as she was crossing the intersection in the city, she saw the officer running down the middle of the street waving his arms to stop her. In his hand was an envelope, her residency.

Louise supported herself solely on her social security. Her church helped with her first ticket to Honduras and often, during the year, would send gifts of money; but basically, it was Louise. Her social security provided her with around $600 each month. This and her small stipend from the school (usually $30 to $50 worth of gas and food) was what she lived on. Things were much cheaper there, so she lived well on very little and still managed to help where needed.

You had to know how the system worked. Unless it was a matter of life or death, you never saw anything. To do so was to put yourself in harm's way, or in a position where you would have to bribe your way out of a situation. These were poor people, but they were survivors, not ignorant, and masters at manipulating money from North Americans. In their minds, if you were from the north, you had money—even if you didn't.

This was true not only in accidents but also matters involving drugs. To talk was to be dead. She would often hear the planes, especially in the night, landing to refuel there on the North Coast for the second half of their flight from Colombia to Florida. More than once, she saw the little plastic-wrapped packages floating in the water. "*Nunca toca*,"[15] she was advised, quietly.

She was sitting at a table on the beach with friends one Saturday afternoon, in the area of the cantinas. A taxi pulled out onto the sand, then another. A large black man got out of the second taxi, gold necklaces catching the sun, heavy rings flashing on his chunky fingers. He had that "don't mess with me" look and was backed up by two gun-toting bodyguards. He met the first taxista. They talked. Some merchandise was loaded by the guards, and a large envelope given to the taxi driver.

"He's selling drugs," said Louise, too loud.

"Ssh," said her friend.

Her years dispatching at the sheriff's office bounced to the fore, and she insisted, "But it's drugs. Where are the police?" She started to get up.

A strong hand grabbed her arm and pulled her down, hard.

---

[15]   never touch

"Louisa, *silencio*," he hissed, his eyes glaring at her.

"But—" she started.

He got up, took her arm, and they walked out past the buildings to the street.

"Louisa, you didn't see a thing. You could be killed if you say anything. They will find you one morning with your throat cut." She knew what he was saying. She had seen the police early some mornings, clustered around a body lying in the street.

"But the police—" she started again.

"They know."

She stood there, feeling a little silly for overreacting. He smiled and took her arm. "This is not like your country, Louisa."

She had heard the talk and knew drugs were everywhere, but this was the first time she had actually witnessed something. She learned her lessons hard, this North American teacher, such as trusting others from the north.

One couple, especially, had befriended her. They were a handsome twosome—she was middle-aged, blonde, pretty, and he was outgoing and friendly.

They traveled a great deal, and the husband jokingly remarked he was not welcome in Las Vegas. He had taken the casinos for too much money. At the restaurant one evening, Louise commented to the woman, "It must be nice to travel back to the States to see your children so much. You are a lucky lady."

She stopped at the Casa Azul a few days after the visit. Francine took her aside. "Did you hear about our Canadian friends?" she asked.

"No," answered Louise.

"Interpol picked them up yesterday. She's been running drugs back and forth to the States, and he was wanted for murder in Canada."

Louise was shocked. "Good heavens," she said. "They seemed so nice." She looked at Francine. Again, she felt the need for caution.

When Louise returned to the States that summer, she was not well. A week prior to her trip, she had been to graduation and stopped with friends for a relaxing drink on the little beach *cancha*[16] at the local tourist hotel. Leaning back in the chaise, she was thoroughly enjoying the vista of the moon over the water, so peaceful after the long, tiring day.

A huge mosquito buzzed her head, determined to make her his evening meal. She swatted him several times and finally leaned back, feeling victorious in their little battle. Too late, she felt the sting on her back. She killed him and thought no more about it.

The pain in her head the next morning was unreal. She couldn't stand. It hurt to open her eyes. She was chilled and knew she had a fever. Her head throbbed. She lay curled up in bed, finally crawling to the bathroom on her hands and knees. The pain was terrible. She wanted to die, and quickly. She stayed in bed all that day and night. Toward noon the following day, her neighbor Marcia knocked on her door.

"Are you all right, Louise? I haven't seen you."

"No. I'm sick. It's my head." She didn't move from the bed.

Marcia came in and felt her head, looking worried. "Can you eat something?"

"Oh no. No."

"Are you thirsty?"

---

[16]   lounge

"No. My head hurts so badly."

Marcia left and came back with a glass of water and a spoon.

"Can you drink this?"

"No. It hurts to move my head."

Marcia took the spoon and slowly fed Louise some sugar water. Bit by bit, she downed enough to put back some of the liquids that had burned out.

"Louise, I am going to go to my house and cook you a piece of hamburger, well done, as I know you like it. You have to eat something."

"I don't think I can."

She came back with a plate and a piece of hamburger, cooked as she knew Louise liked it. Louise slowly chewed one small bite, then another. She was not a meat eater, but years later, she could still remember the wonderful aroma of that piece of hamburger.

By the next day, she could stand a few minutes, but her head still throbbed unmercifully. She knew she was sick but was afraid that if she could not make her flight, she would be detained in some infirmary, hospital, or even quarantined. She had to get back home. Marcia packed her clothes, and her landlord, Mr. Connors, took her to his home in La Lima, close to the airport, where she stayed with his family for the night.

She was so miserable she could hardly stand, and called her daughter Candy in Montana. "I'm not coming home well," she said. The pain in her head was dull, agonizing, and relentless.

The next morning, they took her to the airport. "You have to walk straight until you get through the gate," Mr. Connors advised. She nodded and stood, trying as hard as she could to stay upright: one step, then another.

"Yes?" the immigration agent looked at her and smiled.

Louise handed over her ticket, passport, and fee for leaving the country.

"You don't look well, Miss," said the woman.

Louise lied. "I have a serious problem with my eyes. I'm going to a specialist in the States."

"Buen viaje,"[17] the agent said and stamped the passport. Louise moved on. She couldn't stand. She kept falling to the left. Following a wall was good, but when she was in the open, she fell sideways. Finally, she got to her seat to wait. When the call came for the flight, she stationed herself on the right side of the group walking to the plane. As she fell to the left, people kept pushing her back, frowning at her.

"Is she drunk?" they whispered. She got pushed back four or five times. The passengers were not happy with her. As she came to the steps, she was relieved. There was a handrail, and her arms were good.

Houston was a problem. She managed to get to the lines at immigration, but her eyes wouldn't stay open. She fought to stay awake; it was impossible. Putting down her big suitcase, she curled up on it, there in the middle of the line.

"Wake up, lady. You can't lie down here!" She opened her eyes and looked way up at the tallest, biggest officer she had ever seen. A security woman was with him.

The woman took her hand and felt her wrist. "She's cold and clammy," she whispered, alarmed. "We need to get her out of here." She must have thought Louise couldn't hear.

They asked for her passport and ticket. She gave it to them. A wheelchair appeared, and she was whisked away—not to an infirmary but to a seat at the gate for her next flight, Denver.

---

[17]   good trip

Denver was the same story. On the shuttle to the hotel, she kept falling into the other passengers, all of which were flight crews on layover. She kept apologizing, and they just looked at her with disgust.

Her daughter Connie had called her brother-in-law, who came to check on Louise and take her to dinner. She was out of it, babbled and jabbered, didn't eat, and knew she was really not with the program, but there wasn't a thing she could do about it.

When her flight was a half hour out of Billings, she made her way to the restroom and tried to put on some lipstick and comb her hair. She had to look good for her girls.

She felt her way down the Jetway and came out to greet two of her three daughters—Connie, who had driven from North Dakota, and Candy from Lewistown. There was total shock on their faces. They recovered quickly, explaining later her one eye was drooping down, and all in all, she looked sick. Very sick. Going home with Candy was not an option. Instead, it was the hospital. They had already called her doctor. A fantastic physician and diagnostician, he took a high spinal tap. She was isolated, put to bed, and immediately went to sleep.

The next morning, she got the news: viral encephalitis. Brain fever. They call it sleeping sickness. There was no medicine to give for it. Just get well. And she did. Her eyes and her legs were still weak, but she was able to move, walk, and use her body. She was surprised to learn this disease was not confined to warmer climates. Hospitals up on the Milk River in Montana were full of those victims whose limbs would not move. She had been infected by that big black mosquito that also carries malaria and dengue fever.

She healed during the summer and returned to Tela late that August, just in time for classes to begin. She thought of how over thirty of her students' parents had come to visit her just before school ended, presenting her with a petition they had all signed, requesting she come back to teach their children that next year.

It was good to be back.

CHAPTER 4

It was in the fall, before the big hurricane. Louise had stopped at the Casa Azul after school for a sandwich and was talking with a friend when the tall mariachi came by. She had seen him on the streets often, usually laughing with children or talking with friends, and noticed he always smiled and enjoyed people. Her friend greeted Chon and hired this good mariachi to play her a song. When the friend left for the restroom, Chon said, "This one is for you from me," and played "*El Rancho Grande.*"

He found her the next evening, and they talked in the rain. She would see him waiting for her at the compound gate at the end of her school day. She was still living in the five-cottage compound on the beach. They would walk the beach to town together, and the friendship grew.

She knew she had to be careful. Hondurans were very poor; this was the second poorest country in this hemisphere, and any one of them would sell their soul to be involved with a North American. Nevertheless, he made her happy. She was probably very vulnerable, but after teaching those long hot days, it was so nice to walk and relax with him. He didn't push the relationship. He just smiled and was always there. She used to laugh and say he appeared from nowhere.

She often walked the beach by the ocean. This was how she recharged herself—those refreshing rolling waves splashing against her feet and legs, the quiet rhythm, the gentle breeze. She loved this time, but it was dangerous. There were many robbers. Yet when she looked, there was

Chon, up near the line of hotels and restaurants, silently watching her, protecting her.

Her free time was short, and her quiet times few. She claimed the air there on the beach was charged, alive with energy. It surged through her, and she found peace. She was hands-off to the local *ladrones*.[18] The word in town was that Chon was good with a knife, and he always carried one. People respected that. But she was still cautious—always cautious.

Back in Montana, this old stuffed bear was unpacked and crammed into a blue carry-on suitcase. Candy's family was going to meet Louise for a vacation in Cancún, and Laura Jane, Louise's granddaughter, carried me all the way. She smiled that beautiful smile, handed her grandmother the handle to the luggage, and I was finally reunited with my Louisa.

On the return trip to Honduras, I flew in the little upper compartment. But in San Pedro Sula, when Chon met us, I had a special seat on the bus—the little bus that stopped every mile or so and carried folk from one small town to another. Louise thought all the little ones would be happy to see me. Not so. They were afraid and moved away. She quickly set me behind her. The smiles cautiously came back.

These were the good people—the "real people," Louise called them—from the farms and mountains; where life is simple and slow; where the men rule, work, and visit the cantinas; where the women cook, clean, and have babies, many babies; where nothing is thrown away; where families are most important and usually all live together; where people help one another; where death is common; where the birth of a new life is cherished by everyone; and where one wonders, *Is this how it is supposed to be? Simple. Easy.*

Acceptance is the word. Life, death, sickness, happiness, adversity, and hunger are all accepted—but with such a strong faith, a faith that tomorrow will be better, surreal.

---

[18]   robbers

Hurricane Mitch hit Honduras on the twenty-seventh of October in 1998, late for the hurricane season but with a force and duration that knocked the socks off the little country. It churned around and around off the North Coast for six days, blasting the inland with wind and rain. Seven thousand were killed outright; another six thousand were declared missing and never found. Many were buried under the mud in *pueblos*,[19] mountains literally fell, buildings collapsed, raging torrents of water swept away cement and flesh alike—nothing was spared.

Elizabeth came running, talking excitedly in her fast, clipped British accent, "Louisa, they say there is a hurricane coming. What will we do?"

"Oh dear! Find shelter, I guess," Louise answered, her mind racing, thinking of where she could go. She knew she had to leave her beach cabaña because of a possible storm surge. Her cabaña sat on the bank of a large river that flowed into the ocean in front of the compound.

"I think I shall go to Margo's home on the other side of the city," continued Elizabeth. "Where will you go?"

"I'm going to check with Luc and Veronique. They'll know what to do," Louise answered.

"Take care, Louisa," Elizabeth said, already starting up the steps of her cabaña to pack.

Louise pulled me off the couch, along with a few paintings and special personal possessions, and put us in the back of her pickup. She called another neighbor, Sharlene, a tall young Canadian teacher who lived in the cabaña behind her. They jumped into the pickup, left the beach, and stayed that first night with Luc and Veronique, a French couple modernizing an older hotel. The second night was spent at the Maya Vista, a hotel built high on a hill and owned by Pierre and Suzanne, friends from Quebec.

---

[19] villages

They returned to the cabañas the next day, sure the storm would soon end. Winds were frighteningly strong. At times they would lessen, only to begin again, churning up the ocean, dumping tons upon tons of water on the mountains, causing more floods and mudslides that devoured absolutely everything in their path.

Early that afternoon, she felt something banging into her porch. A launch had been left tied to the dock, close to her steps. Winds were lifting it, whipping it out into the river then throwing it back through the fence into her porch and steps. A few more thrusts and the corner of her house would fall.

She grabbed a kitchen knife and called Sharlene for help. Pushing against the wind and dodging the whipping boat, she inched her way out to the dock and sliced the rope. The launch swung around to the middle of the river, upended, and sank. Sharlene left to find other shelter, and as Louise fought against the wind and climbed back up the two sets of steps, she saw the heavy cement lid of the septic tank skidding down the road. She struggled back into the cabaña and safety.

The roar of the storm increased even more. She looked out through the fierce wind and driving rain toward the ocean where huge waves were surging toward shore. One after another they would rise up, stand suspended for a moment, and fall back—again and again, each time stronger than before. Her eyes caught three men holding on to the large fence posts around the compound. They had taken their belts, fastened themselves to the posts, and there they waited, watching for Louise to leave the compound. By now, all the residents had moved away from the ocean, and once she was gone, everything would be theirs.

Winds strengthened. The roar reminded her of Niagara Falls. Palms were bent to the point of snapping. The men strapped to the posts used their arms to shield their heads from flying debris. She was getting uneasy. Night was coming, and no electricity meant no lights.

She heard a banging on the door and a voice calling, "Louisà! Louisà!" It was Chon, his machete in one hand and his guitar in the other. She brought him inside where he announced, "You have no father or brother, and your family is not here, so I will take care of you." She thought of the men outside, the roar of the hurricane, and the ever-rising water.

"*Gracias.*" She was thankful and relieved.

Chon and his machete stood guard outside her door, in plain sight of the ladrones, the entire evening and into the night. The men finally left, but Chon still stood firm. In the morning, when the winds lessened, he and Louise tried to move some of the debris. A huge palm had fallen across the driveway, and several natives offered to move it if they could have the coconuts and the heart. Their families were hungry. This would sustain them.

Toward evening, as the increasing winds were bringing the ocean even closer, she and Chon discussed leaving. Her new knee made walking risky. Chon explained how dangerous it would be to go out. The metal sheets of lamina on the roofs in the compound were blowing off. Being hit by one could slice a person in half. Another endless day came and went.

Surely, this would leave soon. It had been five days. But it didn't.

That last night, she pushed the door open to sheer horror—the deafening roar and the ocean, right there at the top step, inches below her floor, black waves rolling in onto her feet as though they were trying to grab her. The wind was impossible to push against. Chon helped her close the door. I had gotten wet from the rain blowing in, and she put me in the corner of the sofa.

At midnight, it was worse. The water was at the door, dark and menacing, the wind pushing it in underneath. She looked at Chon. "Es okay, Louisà. Es okay," he said, trying to reassure her.

We should have gone yesterday, she thought to herself.

They heard a portion of the metal roof blow away. There was nothing to do, nowhere to go. It was pitch-black, and there they were, high in a one-room cabaña with the ocean and the thunderous roar of the hurricane all around them. *Please, God,* her mind screamed, *please help us.*

They half-sat together on the edge of the old brown plastic sofa. She reached over and pulled me close to her. It was the end. She knew they would be blown away by the next powerful gusts rocking the whole structure. Chon put his arms around her and held her close, and they waited.

Then she felt it, ever so slightly. It was lessening. Unbelievable. She was afraid it would start again. Gradually, it slowed. It was moving out. It had begun to work its way back up the coast. Six days of pure hell. And then it was over. *Thank you,* her thoughts poured out. *Thank you, thank you, thank you.*

At sunup, they opened the door to a rainy calm and ground covered with piles of debris and sand blown down from the city and swept in by the sea. A baby pelican was resting on the bottom step, disoriented and lost. They began clearing a path to the gate to put the baby out on the beach, hoping its mother would find it. Sand and garbage covered everything; piles were almost two feet high. She tried clearing sand off some of her plants; there was just too much.

She drove down to the city where the barges were coming in. Children and oldsters, devoid of all expression, were being carried to benches. They had hung in trees for days, along with ants and snakes, all desperately clinging to life. Every ambulance was busy. Dr. Christina asked Louise to help transport victims—first to the clinic to be treated for bites and a host of other maladies, then to the different schools where they would be housed and fed.

Louise finally found a phone line open to the States. It would only accept collect calls; that was fine. She had to let her family know she was okay. The relief on the other end of the phone was instantaneous. "Yes, yes, of course, I'll accept it!"

She told Candy she would get a letter out as soon as she could. The mail was not going through, but she found a fax machine in the city, and her words brought comfort to her children. They were also printed in her hometown newspaper. Donations began pouring in, and Candy worked with the local priest to get the money to Louise.

Reports reaching Tela were unreal: a cement house filled with thirty people wiped away; dozens killed when an eighteen-foot wave tore down the river at El Progreso, ripping out the big bridge. Tela was completely cut off. Louise found she could get money through her Visa card at the bank and stocked up with enough to fill her pickup with gas and buy food. Vendors knew what she was doing and made sure she had supplies.

Tela was lucky; damage in the little bay was much less than inland. In a few days, food began reappearing and bottled water came via boats. The sewers were working right into the river. Inland, the stench of open sewage and the dead, both human and animal, forced people to keep their faces covered. Cholera, malaria, and other maladies that travel on the tails of a hurricane became a real threat.

Chon had not heard from his family up in Locomapa, a village high in the mountains above Yoro. They waited. Never more apparent was the fact that they were just visitors on this earth for a little while. The sea rolled on, the winds bent the great palms, the warm rains came and went, the ants were busy building a new colony, children were involved in a soccer game, and trees and bushes stripped of their leaves began to show new sprouts of green.

She wrote to her children about the families, such as the one in Arizona, a little village a few miles from Tela, where the man from the rescue boat sat with his head in his hands—remembering; the family was all out on the roof, but the fellows couldn't get to them. The water got higher, the wind blew harder, and one by one, the family disappeared.

Carol, Louise's friend, came to see her, asking for a little help. Louise told her she was extended way past the stopping point, so Carol nodded.

She said her little brother and his wife lived up in the mountains. During the hurricane, they saw the creek rising rapidly. He grabbed her arm and took her across the log. When they got to the other side, the log and their house went down the creek, which had grown to a full raging river in a matter of minutes. He said the house made a horrid popping noise as it broke in two and tumbled from sight.

They struggled up the mountain, down the other side to the road, and caught a ride in the back of a big truck. The truck was sliding badly, and she was being thrown from side to side, so they finally walked, catching rides with other trucks until they got to Yoro, then Progreso, and finally, to Tela. The woman's baby was due in three weeks. They arrived around noon, and she was rushed to the hospital where they took the baby by cesarean section. She was sixteen years old.

Carol made her a few cotton throws, as all the girl had was the dress she had on. In the hospital, there were no sheets or clothes, so they had washed her wet, bloodstained dress and put it back on her. They needed the mattress for other women, so she had to leave the hospital the next day. Friends in the barrio rallied, and there were clothes for the new baby girl.

What Carol needed was help getting the family back home to the mountains. Louise explained she couldn't get away to take her; and even if she could, the road was impassable. She offered to help with the gas if Carol could get someone else to take them. She also said she thought the girl should stay with Carol for two weeks. From the look on Carol's face, she knew this was a hardship. She had little food. Louise found some money for food, helped with the gas back to nothing, and gave the kids 300L to get food when they got home.

She later wrote to her children, "How can you say no?"

CHAPTER 5

Days after the hurricane, Chon was still there. Late one night, Louise woke to find a hand across her mouth.

"Shhhhh," whispered Chon. He crept to the machete that hung inside the door, then silently, to the porch door. "*Que pasò!*"[20] he yelled, leaping out.

There was another man's voice, screaming; both voices were shouting, the machete hitting again and again. The screen door slammed open. The ladrone bounded down the steps and across the compound, followed closely by Chon. Lights were going on in the neighbors' houses. Up over the fence went the robber, pursued by Chon who abruptly stopped, turned, ran back up the porch steps and inside, grabbed some clothes, and grinned.

Neighbor Elizabeth, a missionary from Texas, had been treated to quite a show—a ladrone running across the compound to the fence, being chased by a naked machete-waving Indian. Louise smiled secretly and thanked God Chon was there.

Blood was splattered all over the porch and down the steps. She asked Chon if he was hurt. "No," he said, seriously, "but the ladrone was." She shuddered as she looked at her clothes, shoes, and hammock, all piled neatly on the steps for a quick getaway.

---

[20] What are you doing?

She saw a man in the market weeks later with a bandage across one eye and around his arm and hand. From the way he looked at her, she was sure it was the same poor robber. *This was still third world*, she reminded herself.

After Chon stood watch during the hurricane, he begged and begged to get a *pistola*, and she finally consented. They decided to go to La Ceiba to look for the pistol. It was a bad trip. She could see where the mountains had slid, burying everything in their path.

Huge mahogany trees had been uprooted and tossed like matchsticks, coming to rest between the highway and the mountains. Their massive reddish trunks were interwoven, stripped of the bark, and shoved into formidable barricades running the length of the broken highway. The natural green of the forests had been beaten down, trampled into the mud by monstrous rocks and splintered trees.

Sides of the tall mountains were scarred where boulders had gouged the earth. Wide, vast holes, reaching a hundred yards across, were hauntingly empty after tons of seawater, carried in by heavy clouds, had caused enormous sections of Mother Earth to let go, slide over and smother little *aldeas*[21] and farms.

Bridges in Honduras were out, every one. To get to La Ceiba, it was necessary to drive through the big, wide river. Large baskets run by cables carried people across. The river was too wide and high for cars, but pickups could make it. Louise got in line with her old Ford Ranger. One look at the muddy water rushing by scared her. She geared to low, stepped on the gas, and dropped into the water.

The truck in front of her was in up to its fenders, and she had to begin slowing down. Worried she may lose her momentum, she sat on her horn. The big fellow kept going, and she pulled her little pickup through.

It was raining by that time, and the river was rising fast, becoming a rushing torrent of churning, dirty water. She knew if she was to get back

---

[21]   towns

across, it had to be now, so against Chon's loud objections, she turned around and started back. It was worse.

The man running the big winch truck watched her as she came slowly back through the rampaging high water, and finally, ashore and up the hill. She began to cry; tears of frustration, exhaustion, and stress spilled down her cheeks. Chon's compassion was outweighed by his eagerness for a pistola.

"Why are you crying? We could have gone on."

"But we couldn't have come back."

"Why worry? We could stay in La Ceiba."

She didn't answer, just cried quietly.

He bought a pistol in Tela. Chon was happy. He proudly wore his new weapon tucked into his belt in front, his shoulders a little more square. His status among his friends had gone up a notch.

Recovery after Mitch took months to even begin. Villages were flattened, roads were out, and thousands were living in cardboard or plastic shelters on the highways, camping in schools, and existing any way they could. Relief was coming in but often not getting where it was needed most.

Louise received close to $10,000 from the people of Central Montana after they read the letter she had written home. Her priest in Tela notified her that she should turn any donations over to the church relief fund. Louise found this unacceptable, especially when they said they would decide who needed it and who did not. She refused.

Instead, she took food to the guardaria, barrios near town, and sent supplies to the mountains. When she learned Dr. Christina Rodriguez was heading a group to feed the villages, restore schools and hospitals, and bring medical care, she threw her support behind them.

She took Dr. Christina to the bank where she had set up a separate account. It could not be mixed with her private account.

Teams of women boxed food. Wheelbarrows, building supplies, cement, food, and clothes were loaded into the big longboats and taken upriver to Rio Tinto and El Tìgrè.

All she asked was proof. With so much money at her command, she was compelled to account to the people of her Montana home just where their donations had gone.

The proof came from countless little pueblos thanking her with pictures of work, lists of people—some of each member living there, and receipts. It was all accounted for. She was pleased.

Metzapa was a little town up in the mountains, about fifty miles from Tela. Because she had a covered pickup, she was asked to take a load of food to the little pueblo, which had pretty much been cut off since the hurricane.

She left with a full load of food, two *bomberos*,[22] and a sister from the Catholic school who knew the village and the mountains. As bridges were gone, the seven streams they crossed were forded—first by the soldiers walking across, then the pickup following.

A mudslide moving menacingly down the mountain from high above caused them some concern, but they got across. She closed her mind to going back.

Along a little trail, where the cactus grew alongside the palms and hibiscus, they turned into a clearing set in the center of dense jungle. Not a soul was in sight. The sister got out, took her bullhorn, and spoke in their native dialect.

---

[22] soldiers with machine guns

Several minutes later, some children began emerging from the trees, then a few of the older women. At the sister's calm Spanish, more women began coming forth, some carrying babies on their hips. Louise stayed in the pickup to avoid frightening the people. There were no men in sight.

Soldiers began passing out the packages of food as folks milled around the pickup. A young boy showed Louise a little helicopter he had made from sticks and tried talking with her through the open pickup window. An older toothless woman was showing off her blouse to friends. She had sewn pieces of ribbon on to it, every color and kind she could find.

Still, there were no men. The food was almost all gone by this time, with people still left in line. They divided the packs and finally ran out.

Suddenly, the soldiers were banging on the pickup roof and shouting, "*Salè! Salè!*"[23] The passenger door opened, and the white blur of the sister flew inside. "*Rapìdo! Rapìdo!*" she shouted. Looking up, Louise gasped—from out of the jungle the men were coming towards them— long sharp machetes in their hands.

She tried to start the pickup but killed the motor twice. Again, it died the third time, and panic set in. The soldiers were shouting at her and banging on the cab. Finally, she stomped on the gas, turned the key, and it started.

She revved the motor, shoved it into reverse, and they shot back, then forward, blindly charging up the rise and out down the trail. She didn't stop at the streams, just barreled right across. After the third, they slowed a bit, catching their breath.

Ahead loomed the mudslide. "*Alto,*"[24] they said. The mud had gained momentum and was moving down the mountain much faster than before. The road was nowhere in sight. The sister and the bomberos would not ride, indicating she should walk with them. They said the pickup would not make it.

---

[23]   Go! Go!

[24]   stop

Six months out of a new knee replacement, Louise knew she could not walk through that moving mass of mud, much less to the nearest town. The pickup was her only chance. She shook her head and waited as they moved across, struggling with each step, grasping each other's hands for support. On the far side, they turned back to watch and wait for her, concern clear on their faces.

She looked straight down the mountain to her left. If she went over, no one would ever find her buried in that mud. She prayed out loud as she put the pickup in low and stepped on the gas. *Oh, God, please. Slowly, slowly, not too fast, just let it dig its way across. Please, God.*

That night, when she was safely home in her house with her flowers and dogs, she said to Chon, "I was scared."

He said, "*Sí.* They could have killed you, and no one would have ever known. You should not go again."

Nevertheless, she did, and after that, he usually went with her. Roads and highways in Honduras were dangerous. Robbers waited off the road, dressed in fatigues to resemble the military. They blocked the highway, carjacked, and robbed unlucky travelers—taking their clothing, shoes, papers, money, and jewelry—leaving them totally helpless alongside the road.

Having a man in the vehicle helped, especially one with a pistol. Chon went with her many times, and there were times she was glad to have that pistol around. More prominent people had their own guards, men who rode standing back of the cab, with machine guns. Many had guards at their homes, which were surrounded by a fence, often electric and topped with razor wire.

Louise was teaching fifth grade the year of the hurricane. The first day they were allowed to reopen the school, Louise asked her twenty-four students to write a paper on their personal experiences or those of a family's or friend's during a week that would be remembered as possibly the worst in the history of Honduras. She read their papers, took a few lines from each, and prepared a brochure to send back to the States.

Each wrote from their heart, not afraid to express their emotions. As is true of their culture, the hurricane was referred to in their world as masculine (he).

Aixa wrote: "In the mountains, where the hurricane caused a lot of disaster, there are children that have no family, and there are fathers, mothers, and families that have no children. People who live in Ceiba and La Lima are damnificados because their homes have blown away or are covered with mud."

Rodrigo said: "The hurricane came and stayed and stayed, and the hurricane stopped. My cousin died and my aunt died too, and all my family lost all their houses. Tomorrow my mother will go to Choluteca with food, water, and medicine to my uncle, aunt, and other cousin. My mother said Choluteca was horrible, and my grandmother was crying, and my little cousin was crying too."

Dennis wrote: "The Chiquita Banana was covered with mud. The streets were all crashed in Progreso. My grandfather told me that from parts of San Pedro Sula to Progreso, the land was covered with water and dead animals. In his pass by the Territory Hondureño, Mitch left people dead and crying. He left people with nothing."

From Daniel: "During the seven days, they say that in Tela the waves were up to eighteen feet tall. The coast of Honduras disappeared up to 80 percent. Rivers grew and ate up houses. The International Airport at San Pedro Sula was full of water and mud. Their doors closed and they could not get help. There was mud everywhere."

Christian stated: "When Mitch stopped in the Caribbean, he was getting harder. He left death, people without homes, food, or water, and he left a lot of sickness. He let rivers get out and destroyed the bridges. It was very, very bad because the ocean was outside where it was supposed to stay. All is getting normal, but tonight a lot of people are alone in the city."

And dear little Heidi wrote: "I was very scared, and I prayed to God to protect us, and I was scared for my grandmother and my other grandfather. Our house was saved, but the house of my grandmother was destroyed, and the cow blew, and the chicken house, and grandfather too. But now he has us and lives in the house with us."

Finally, Josè Carlos wrote: "I never saw a hurricane, and I was not afraid, but now I am. We had storms, wind, and the sky was dark. It rained for many days, and the Hurricane Mitch came, so strong, and destroyed many places. The rivers grew, and the buildings, houses, and trees fell down. I hope in ten years, when I am twenty years, Honduras will be a very pretty country again."

Louise also had a letter of thanks to write to the countless friends and organizations who gave so that she could keep providing help where it was needed. She tearfully drafted a message where she told them her heart was full, and she thanked each one. Their money had made the difference to so many, and in so many ways.

She told them they were there when the medicine they purchased was passed out in Triumfo de la Cruz, Tornabe, San Juan, El Tigrè, and Rio Tinto. They were with her in the guardaria when she held homeless children on her lap, trying to make them more secure; and they bought gas to cook the little ones' supper. They were there when ninety bags of food were passed out in Tolor de Dentro, up in the mountains, after a harrowing two-hour drive through mudslides and rivers where bridges were gone.

Her words reminded them that they would be present that weekend when she would go to El Tigrè's fifteen villages with machetes, shovels, clothes, medicine, and food; that they had been with her at countless doors as she gave out bags of beans, rice, lard, flour, salt, candles, etc. They had filled the gap until other help could arrive.

She shared with them how their hearts should be warm from the smiles of little old women as they walked away with their sacks of food on their heads, or a toothless fellow with sad eyes that lit up when he was given a machete to work with and food for his niños, and a little nine-year-old boy who clutched at a teddy bear she gave him, tears running down his face as she said good-bye. His teeth were clenched shut, and he spoke through them with fear from the flood.

She thanked them again for being there for her and reiterated her pride in her country, the USA, for their immediate aid.

There was a loud rattle at the gate one night weeks after the hurricane. Chon had come back from work early and answered it. "Louisà," he called. She went down to see what he wanted.

He introduced her to a distant cousin of his from the mountains. The fellow was the *patronata*[25] of his village and said he had forty sick people who needed help. He had walked the twenty-seven kilometers to the highway, then caught a ride from one broken segment of pavement to the next, on to Santa Rita, to El Progreso, and heard that maybe this teacher in Tela (meaning Louise) could help him.

Louise called Dr. Christina at her home. The doctora said to meet her down at the clinic right away. They piled into the pickup, drove to the city and the clinic, next to the school. Dr. Christina was already there. She had the doors opened, and as the guard let them in, she was taking bottles off the shelves.

"We will color-code the medicine for men, women, children, and by age," she said.

Louise saw she was taking all the medicine from the shelf. "You need to save some for your patients, Christina," she said.

"Mrs. Langford," said the doctora, "sick people are sick people, no matter where they may be." And she continued marking the medicine.

The patronata would not spend the night, wanting to get back as soon as possible. He had a long way to go. Chon asked if there were other things they needed. He smiled and said sadly, "Everything."

---

[25]   head, leader

He told Chon they had no food, little water, no warm blankets or boots, and that the *Cruz Rojo*[26] had given them machetes but asked for them back after a few days to pass on to other villages. Louise thought of the money she had received and told him to come back. She could help him.

He thanked them, packed the medicine in long bags—the kind that fit on the sides of burros—and left.

Louise contacted a friend from Canada who had also offered money. Together they went to the city. A visit to the Chinaman's shop put together all the items the patronata needed. A week later, he returned with a helper, a young fellow named Francisco who had not seen his parents since they left him with family in the mountains and moved to the valley eighteen years before. He spoke with Chon, and Chon looked at Louise. She knew what he wanted and nodded. She would take them in her pickup.

Francisco had enough money to purchase two pieces of cake. He held the little white box in his hands as Louise drove him and Chon to Rio Leòn, forty miles toward La Ceiba. He and Chon talked in a clickety-clack mountain tongue, animated and full of laughter. At the river, he got out and took a boat for the short ride to see his parents. An hour later, he returned—happy and ready to return to the mountains.

Back in Tela, they loaded the forty blankets, forty pairs of boots, food, medicine, clothes, and three dozen machetes into the same long burro bags, and the men left for the tiring trek home.

It took years before things began improving in the ravaged little country of Honduras. Saltwater had ruined the soil. Crops were gone, villages had to be dug out, land cleared, roads and bridges rebuilt, homes and businesses repaired, and lost families found. The world responded, and life began to get back to semi-normal.

---

[26]   Red Cross

Chapter 6

Louise sold her home in Lewistown. While working relief projects after Hurricane Mitch in and around Tela, she came across some land in Barrio Monte Fresco near her friend Carol. An unfinished cement-block structure sat in the center of the land. She decided to take some of the money from her house sale and build a little home.

"Does anyone know of a carpenter I can get?" she asked at the school.

There was a rap on her classroom door early the next day. "Teacher!" Angel, Giancarlo's father, stepped into the room.

"Yes, Angel?"

"I will make your house," he announced.

"Wonderful."

"But I need to tell you, I will make it much higher. Then you will not get water."

"How much higher, Angel?"

"At least five feet, Teacher."

She agreed. It sounded like a lot, but he knew the area, and it was often flooded. She set the limits, stressing the fact she wanted it simple, basic, and cheap as possible. He nodded. Whenever Angel saw something he did not like, or if she suggested something he didn't approve of, he would say, "Oh, Teacher, it is so *ogly* [long *o*]."

What began as a small home became a big house. She told Angel and the workmen she wanted it all open, completely opposite from the many tiny rooms of the Hondurans. They laughed and called her the *loca gringa*[27] who built a house with no rooms.

From my little stool on the landing of the stairs, everything was in my sight. There were two floors and an open staircase. She could always tell if anyone was there when she stepped in the door.

It was all painted white. The big beams supporting the second floor were stained dark, as was the staircase and trim—striking in its simplicity. An artisan in El Progreso made her furniture of wicker with the high curved back, the kind one sees in pictures. The carpets were some she had purchased a year before at a good price from a salesman from Mozambique, Africa, who was dumping his stock. They were silk and lovely.

All in all, Louise was quite pleased with her home, even though it was much larger than she needed. She was on the edge of the city, and her backyard connected to the wild area, which led to the mountains.

Her neighbors were, for the most part, friendly, but she soon learned Hondurans don't visit much. They did their work and then rested in the heat of the day. After that, there was always more work. Her friend, Carol, lived up one block and over one block—just right to be close friends, yet keep private lives. It was a perfect situation.

People in the barrio didn't "coffee." Louise invited a neighbor for coffee on a Saturday morning. Her husband brought her, stood outside the gate, and told Louise his wife had to sit on the veranda outside. He allowed her to stay fifteen minutes.

---

[27] crazy North American woman

This country was a macho society. It was also third world, and as such, it festered abuse of all kinds—sexual, spousal, animal—all prevalent and often considered normal. Certainly, they weren't all this way. There were many good men, but they were raised to believe the man was the most important. In the mountains, dogs were often more important than women, again depending on the man and how good a cook the woman was.

Louise had to be careful not to say anything to incite problems. She was constantly aware of this, both in school and at home. It was like walking a tightrope, but she did it by focusing on other ways and trying to set an example.

After we moved from the cabaña to our big house, a city employee saw a good thing and managed to acquire the land next to us, used our cement fence as a back wall and built a small house, or so he said. It turned out to be a billiards parlor, open on all four sides, with loud music and lots of smoke and noise. It was horrible.

Louise asked them to turn the sound down. Two minutes later, it was louder than ever. Becoming desperate, she would stand with her hose *watering the flowers* next to the holes in the cement wall, close to the pool tables. When the water got close, the men would turn down the music. It worked once or twice, but that couldn't continue, so she and Carol went door to door with a petition to close the billiards.

A rattle at the gate one Saturday morning brought Louise outside. There was a great deal of noise coming from the street in front.

A tall dark-eyed woman introduced herself: "Hello, my name is Jean Valentine, and I've come to meet the crazy gringa who is causing all this commotion. Did you know the television cameras are outside and your neighbor is telling them how crazy you are?"

Then she threw back her head and laughed. That is how Louise met Jean, and again, her life deepened. It was through Jean that Louise met the people who were the heart of the country. It was a positive, good, and rewarding friendship.

Eventually, the neighbor had to close his billiards with its open sides and loud music and turn it into a home. His wife was a teacher in the government schools and was told she couldn't teach if her husband owned a pool hall. Louise looked up toward heaven, and I heard her say, "Thank you!"

It was about noon on a Saturday. Louise heard motors outside, heavy equipment sounds, and a clanging of her gate lock. Several men stood waiting.

"*Hola*,"[28] she greeted them and opened the gate.

They entered, informing her they were there to make a road to the highway back beyond her house. It would mean they needed to demolish her cement fence on two sides and take the front half and one side of her house.

She blinked. "What? You can't do that!" She wasn't sure of her Spanish, but she was sure they understood.

"Ah, yes, señora. We have the machine here now."

"But I have *domiño plano* on my land."

He frowned. "No, señora. No one in Monte Fresco has domiño plano on their land."

She asked them to wait, went in, found her papers filled with the large colorful stamps, took them out, and showed him. He talked with his friends, turned to her, and said, "I'm sorry, señora. We will have to go check on this in the city. If this is correct, we cannot put the road here."

Thank God I was home, she thought as they left.

That afternoon, her lawyer, Alan, stormed, "Louisa, never let them in the gate. Did they have badges?"

---

[28] Hello

"No."

"They were probably just trying to get money. You should have called me. And never show your papers. If they had torn them or taken them, you would have no proof of anything."

She felt totally deflated.

As I sat in the corner watching in this hot unfamiliar world, I tried to see through her eyes, to read her mind, to understand what she felt and witnessed as she trudged through life in another culture, another world. I listened when she sorted things out in the sanctity of her home; and often, she threw words at me in frustration and despair, relieving the burden of being misunderstood. When she had worked it out in her mind, she set off again to begin anew. That was my service all those years, and what I am passing on to you.

Chon cut the grass in the yard with his machete, kept it short, and raked—important in this country of snakes and other little critters. She often gave him extra money for helping out. Judging by what I saw from my vantage point on the stairs, I am sure he loved her; but he also knew he had fallen into a good life, and he wasn't about to lose it.

A master with the machete, he could flick an ant off a tree branch without touching the bark, and he had the power to take off a palm frond with a single swipe. Louise tried to trim the bushes but only succeeded in chopping them up. "Sorry," I would hear her say to the poor branches. Machetes are heavier than they look, and it took practice. She finally learned.

Snakes terrified her, but she learned to accept life with the spiders and scorpions. Chon moved a box one morning by the back door, yelled, and jerked his hand away.

"Louisà," he said quickly, "find the scorpion." She was more interested in the bite. "No! Find the scorpion!" he shouted. She finally found it.

He stepped on its body, cut off the stinger at the end of the tail, and quickly slapped the crushed scorpion against the bite.

She stood, gaping at him. "There is antivenom in their body," he explained.

He was right. The next day, the red was nearly gone.

If it wasn't snakes, scorpions, or spiders, it was ants—horrid tiny fire ants that could turn a foot or a leg into excruciating pain, and the migrating army ants that marched through her house once a year in a two-to-three-inch swath.

Evidently, she built the house on their path. Spraying only killed the front ones. The rest marched over the dead and continued the trek. Guard soldiers would stand on their back feet at each side of the line, warning not to get close. They really worried her, but she found that if she waited twenty minutes, they would be gone for another year.

Last but equally frightening were the big ants, up to three-quarters of an inch long. She knew they were in the walls, but other than that, they never bothered. The sight of them was enough to scare her away. She was more afraid of ants and snakes than anything.

Chon worried about Louise. On a rainy day, he walked over two miles to the school to take her a sweater. He knew she would be cold. And I, from my special place on the landing, would see her get him things he needed and always slip him some money. They were good for and to each other.

I remember the handsome tall mariachi, the teacher, and the caring and happiness. It was beautiful. He was so attentive. He worshipped her. I sat on a miniature stool on the landing of the stairs where I could see the doors, the kitchen, and hear every little sound.

When Chon came in, he took off his white shirt and put it on the back of the chair to dry. He always wore a T-shirt under it no matter how hot. Chon was proper. He was also a woodsman and came from high in the mountains above Yoro—one of the *Tulepanes,* an indigenous people of that region.

To get to his family home, he took the bus as far as possible, to a place called Locomapa. Then it was a ten-to-twenty-kilometer hike straight up the mountains. This was coffee country, with snakes and jungle. There was no running water and little privacy. Louise's request to go up was quickly put to rest. He knew his world, and it was no place for a woman from North America. Women in the mountains were different. It was primitive and basic.

I heard him tell her how his family had a little land high up there where they grew corn and coffee, but he loved the music and finally left to make his living playing his songs. He was good, not the Fernando Hernandez he wanted to be, but he had the voice and personality people liked. He came alive in front of an audience. Chon loved people and never knew a stranger.

In his work on the boulevard in the city, along the beachfront and the big hotels, Chon knew well the little beggar boys (called the Chiclets Boys because they sold Chiclets gum). Most were orphaned or runaways, and none went to school.

At the house, he took his machete and some boards and constructed a very crude but ingenious little box. It was tall, about twelve inches. A flap opened on either side, and the inside held tools—shoeshining tools. The flat, narrow top served as a shoe rest. He took it to the city, and a friend made three more.

They were filled with shoe polish and cloths and presented to four of his little followers. It was a great moment. They shined away, snapping the cloths, big smiles on their faces, and became proud. For Chon, it was a feeling of satisfaction as he steered Louise through the crowds to watch his boys at work.

Louise often wondered if she would have survived if it had not been for Chon. He was named Purificaciòn Rivera Cruz. His twin sister was also named Purificatiòn. She was called Pura, and he, Chon.

He was quiet, respectful, but had a presence. He was tall for a Honduran, handsome, with big twinkly dark eyes and that ready smile, which said *friend.* He wore a white shirt, black pants, and a Western hat. A traditional red mariachi bow at his neck completed his outfit.

He loved playing his big old guitar and was equally as good on the accordion. He would rather play than talk and was happiest when he was belting out traditional Honduran folk songs, the old fellows sitting in the cantinas singing along. It was his happiness. He was a born entertainer and could bring his countrymen together in song like a true maestro.

The chemistry between Louise and Chon was uncanny. He was her soul mate. She could always feel his presence. "Chon is coming," she would say to the birds, and sure enough, the gate would rattle, and they would hear his whistle.

He never came to the house without a little bag of fruit of some kind— bananas, mangos, melon, or cantaloupe. And he always entered the gate with a whistle. That is, unless he was angry because she wouldn't give him money. Then he was silent. Not a word. This was a macho nation. Men made the rules. No matter the situation, they would make a rule. Sometimes the words hurt enough to bring tears, but it was soon over.

When there was a problem, or if she just needed to talk, there was always Carol. She was Louise's friend, one of the first people Louise met when she came to Tela. Carol raised her four children by doing other people's washing, ironing, cooking, cleaning, and by teaching kindergarten at the same school where Louise taught. She learned English after she came down from the mountains, from the woman she first worked for—her aunt.

She lived in a small cement-block house with potted flowers all around her porch. Part of the support beams in the roof had collapsed, and several iguanas lived up there. Louise would usually find her preparing lessons, sitting outside in a big porch chair to catch the breeze. She would see Louise drive up, come down the steps to the pickup, open the door, grab the hand bar to lift her heavy body into the seat, and say, "What's up?"

She was one of those special people who could turn a room into happy when she came in. She had lots of troubles, mostly money, and also asthma, due partly to her weight—but she still smiled. She was always a comfort to Louise.

"Don't let him see you cry, and don't answer him," she would say. "He's like those mountain men. Just wait." She went on, "We're different up there. It's another world, my friend. Just don't push. I know him. It's his way. He believes he is right. He doesn't think he's wrong. He thinks you are." Her quiet wisdom was unbelievable and always right. Carol knew because Carol came from the same area.

She told of how she escaped from the mountains—of how, when her husband came home, he yelled at her and threatened her. She would always be humble until that final time. She ran. I saw her show Louise the seven big scars on her arms, legs, and body where he cut her with his machete before she got away.

Carol said she ran as hard as she could, straight down that steep mountain. She knew if she fell she would be killed; if she stopped and he caught her, she would also be dead; and like she said, dead is dead, so she ran faster.

When she got to the bottom and the highway, she jumped in the back of a moving pickup, ended up in El Progreso, and finally, Tela. She lived in a little house on the outskirts. She had a son and, later, three more children; but she never remarried. There were times she would laugh and say, "We had *platanos* for three days. I boiled them for breakfast and fried them for supper." She knew Louise would give her some money for a little food. Carol was prudent—too prudent—but that's how she survived.

Oftentimes, after giving her money, Louise would hear a rattle at the gate. Carol's grandchildren would say, "Come, Teacher," and take her back where she would find the neighborhood gathered, ready to enjoy a huge pot of rice and vegetables. Each one had contributed what they had, and together, it made a meal for all—but not until she joined them.

The gate clanked one afternoon. It was Carol. Louise liked Carol's visits, but this time she could tell there was something on Carol's mind.

"I may need some help," Carol volunteered.

"How?"

"My two nephews are coming to live with me. My sister wants them to go to school, and they can't in the mountains. The husband put them out, and she and the two boys, ages seven and ten, are living in the field. I told her I would take them for a while." She stopped, looking a little embarrassed.

"What can I do?" asked Louise

"I need to take them to town for some clothes and shoes—maybe to the Chinaman's shop."

Louise didn't hesitate. "Of course, what day?"

"They will be here tomorrow. Maybe we could go Saturday. I'll see they have clean clothes and something on their feet."

Saturday morning, Louise drove up to Carol's. The boys were standing on the porch—two scrubbed little bodies, hair slicked down, and flip-flops on their clean feet.

They stared at Louise as Carol ushered them into the backseat. They rode silently, still staring at her. They answered no questions and said not a word, but their eyes were big as saucers. Finally, as they pulled up in front of the Chinaman's shop, Carol said, "You'll have to forgive them, Mrs. Langford. You see, they've never seen a white woman, they've never ridden in a car, they've never seen a woman drive, they've never heard English, and they've never been in a city."

One child clasped firmly in each hand, Carol took them into the *tienda*. Shoes were first on the list. The salesman tried to take off the flip-flops. No. The little one was stubborn. He finally had shoes, and no one was going to take them off—until he saw the new shoes. The socks went on, then the new shoe. His eyes popped, and a smile spread from ear to ear. The problem was the shoe was too small. The salesman brought a larger size. There was no way that smaller shoe was coming off. He was a strong little fellow. It took all three adults to change one shoe.

Shirts and trousers came next. After the Chinaman was paid, they piled back into the car. The ride home was happier. The boys stayed for several months. Their mother went to the courts, and she and the children were put back into the house. Louise questioned her return, but Carol simply said, "She's a fool."

Honduras is a strange country. Many marry, many don't. Many men have several women, and some are loyal to one. Things that would shock Louise at first, she found to be part of their culture. On the other hand, things she found customary in her country were often questioned there.

She tried to understand Chon's culture. A big problem was the beer and the *guaro*.[29] Men from the mountains would gather at the local cantina for camaraderie and to relax. Home was where they went for food and sleep, but the local cantina was their meeting place with their *paisanos*.[30] After he left the mountains, Chon's mariachi work was usually with the drinking public and in the company of fellow mariachis. Alcoholism plagued him as it did a great percentage of his paisanos, be it in the mountains, towns, or cities.

[29] native liquor

[30] countrymen

With his keen hearing, Chon could pick up the early-morning mating whistle of the feared barba amarilla,[31] an extremely dangerous and aggressive snake, which would slide through the jungle in back of her house. His awareness was like having a radar system guarding her home. Still, they were vulnerable. They needed something more, and the neighbors took care of that.

The little barrio decided Louise needed a dog—a must in Central America. They bark and are usually mean and extremely protective. Late one afternoon, several neighbors came to the gate, one of them holding a tiny two-week-old puppy that fit into the palm of Louise's hand. His mother had been bitten by a snake and died, leaving three small pups. That is how we got Buddy.

He was a beautifully marked hound. The yellow flowered sheet she had salvaged from a friend became his bed, and Chon helped see he had milk every few hours during those first nights. Their loving care produced a happy, healthy pup that grew to almost three feet high and dug up all the bushes and flowers Louise had so tirelessly brought home and planted.

Chon got out his machete and made wooden stakes of every size and shape to protect all her precious plants. The garden was full of wooden stakes.

Shortly after that, on a Saturday morning, Louise took Chon into the city to work. A quiet little restaurant looked inviting, so they stopped for a *baleada*.[32] It was a peaceful spot, set back in the shade of the palms. Several young boys walked by, playing catch with something that was yipping and crying. Louise grabbed twenty limps and ran out to the street.

"Niños, es su perro?" (Boys, is that your puppy?)

"Si. Es de Josè." (Yes, it's Josè's.)

---

[31]   fer de lance

[32]   flour tortilla filled with beans and cheese

"Josè, veinte limps por el perro. Okay?" (Josè, twenty limps for the puppy. Okay?)

"Si."

She took the shaking puppy and held him close. That's how Igor came to live with us. Buddy taught him well. They chased the iguanas and the *pichetes*.[33] They dug flowers, barked at the sound of her neighbor's motorbike, and protected the house. They were Louise's security.

When she would go out and call "Buddy, Buddy, come here, Buddy," all the neighbors would grin at her.

"Why do they always smile?" Louise asked one day.

Carol chuckled and said, "Mrs. Langford, the word *buddy* in our language means 'varicose veins.'" They laughed and laughed.

The neighbor's boy had brought her a young gray-striped pigeon with a broken leg, and she nursed him back to health. Perky, as she called the little *paloma*, learned to fly; first from the chair to her hand, then back, each time farther and farther until finally, one day, he joined the large group that came daily for corn, and flew away. He returned, along with all his relation, and from then on, each morning at five thirty on the button, a sky full of palomas came for breakfast at Louisa's.

She fed between eighty and a hundred, all frantically trying to get the last kernel. Minutes later, they would fly away. My, how she loved them. She said when you could touch them, they felt like baby powder.

Louise found her first big parrot, Charley, at a friend's home in the mountains. They had brought him in from the woods and, when they saw how much she cared for him, gave him to Louise. He was a large bird, and Louise was thrilled with him. Parrots are very fragile. A year later, he caught cold. She exhausted every remedy she could think of. He died in her arms. She cried as she buried him.

---

[33] little lizards

Buying or selling parrots was illegal. She rescued Dorilla, Paco, Polly, and Pedro when they were brought to her gate. It was big business and sad the way the nests were robbed by men with large, heavy gloves. She told herself the main reason she took them was to save their lives, but she loved the birds.

Polly and Pedro were mean and would bite; only Chon could handle them. But Dorilla and Paco were hers. Dorilla was a green from Nicaragua and talked easily and clearly. Paco was little, pretty, and friendly. Dorilla would eat oatmeal, drink coffee, and talk with Louise each morning. She'd call Louise "Dorissa." If Louise didn't come down early enough, Dorilla would call her loudly. My stool was right above them, and I would hear "Doña, Doña, Dorrriiissa. *Buenos dias*, Dorissa."

She would often sing to Louise about the tears in the flowers, the "*Llores en la Flores*." There were times too when Louise would hear voices downstairs and, after listening closely, find it was Dorilla repeating conversations she had heard. Louise loved her so very much.

Tropics and rain go together. It's warm and refreshing, but there is a great deal of it—torrents. In the evening, after the rain, they began. Hundreds of frogs, each trying to outdo the other, set off a deafening chorus that only seemed to get louder as night came.

Aside from the noise, these frogs were poisonous. Buddy would try to catch them, then get deathly ill from their spray. White foam would drip from his mouth. After several days he got better, but the vet said if he wasn't so big, he would have died. Igor was smarter. He left the frogs alone.

Louise didn't know what to do to with Buddy other than wait it out and hope he stopped chasing them. When she went outside in the evening, she would see the ugly things sitting unmoving on the cement. Then she had an idea—a horrible, cruel idea.

For lack of nothing to watch on television some weekends, she began to follow the golf tournaments. She actually became quite a fan.

Smiling, she went outside, grabbed a board standing by the back door, and approached one of the big, old gray frogs. She took her stance, then the big swing, and *wham!* Old froggie sailed about fifteen feet and fell to earth, flat as a pancake and dead as a doornail.

And so Louise had a new hobby. Each evening, she went out, found a couple of poisonous-looking old frogs, and *wham!* Her aim was pretty good. She knew she should feel bad, but she really didn't. She would look at me with a grin, give me a pat on the head and go on up the stairs.

CHAPTER 7

As she passed the Casa Azul early one Saturday morning, Francine came running out. "Louise, you had a phone call. It's the one you've been expecting. I'm so sorry."

Louise's mother had been deteriorating, and at ninety-three, the end was coming. Louise had no phone, and Francine had given her number to Louise's sister. This was the call she had been dreading. A few months before, in February, Louise had flown to Colorado to visit her mother. Clad in her sweaters and warmest summer clothes, she had flown to Houston and boarded a plane filled with skiers headed for the Colorado slopes. She was glad she had gone. Her mother was failing. Now she was with God.

As much as it is expected, death still hurts—so very badly. Louise sought out the ocean. She sat under the great palms, watched the gentle waves roll by, and grieved for her mother. She was a wonderful woman, always happy, with a most distinctive and infectious laugh. She was also a crusader for any worthy cause, a mother who saw that her two girls were schooled in the social graces and the arts, and a woman whose religious teachings were hands-on.

The family was poor, but there was always chicken when the bishop came, and waffles, eggs, and sausage every Saturday night. At Christmas, she sewed for weeks, and there was a gift under the tree for everyone. She was a good, strong, and capable person and could be a force to reckon with—a good force.

Louise thought of her throughout that day and could hear her wonderful laughter. She walked the ocean, the waves ministering to her soul as they lapped at her feet. She thanked God for her mother and went home to grieve. I saw her walk through the door with her head low, sad again.

Caring people called on her, and Monday, the student body of the school, led by Carol, sang "The Lord's Prayer," dedicated to her mother, Nessie Chambers.

I liked my life there. It was hot. I mean *hot*, but of course, I didn't feel it. I saw Louise, up each morning at five o'clock, showered, dressed, and ready for school and the heat. Chon rose earlier, like in the mountains. He worked late, often until early morning, but was always up before Louise. And when she came down, there would be a hot cup of strong coffee and two big sugar cookies waiting for her at the table. I saw them so very happy. They came from two totally opposite worlds and cultures, and they both tried to understand the other.

By afternoon, when it was so extremely hot, I would see her drag into the house, drop her book bag, and collapse into a chair at the kitchen table. There was always cold water in a pitcher in the *refri*.[34] She would fill a glass, sit, and catch her breath.

Summers in Honduras were so hot there was often a haze over the sun. But around February, it changed. That's when the rains usually began. Basically, this was the only change in the seasons. The deluges often lasted a week or more, rolling in from the sea and blanketing the land.

In my special corner, I sat through many of those torrential downpours— the ones that produced scary floods that would quickly creep up and under the door. Sometimes, little trickles of water would come in the window and drip down my brown bear fur.

During one of those hard storms, the water rose to a little over three feet, and everyone in the barrio was evacuated. Everyone but Louise.

---

[34] refrigerator

Her house was built high, and even though the water lapped at the door and seeped in under it a little, we were dry and had food and water to last the few days until it went down.

Determined to not miss any of her classes, Chon helped Louise walk the four blocks out to the main road. Struggling in water up to her chest was difficult—that along with never knowing what might be swimming toward you, including snakes that were eager to find something to climb up on.

At the bridge, there was a taxi waiting. Walking into the school, she found she was the only one there. During rain like this there was no school. No one left their homes. They feared *gripe*,[35] which in this climate often led to pneumonia.

I remember once, just after a big rain, the water was very high, and Chon was antsy, pacing back and forth on the balcony. His life was in the city, and that's where he wanted to be. As a rowboat came by checking homes, he flagged it down. Five minutes later, he was sitting, barefooted, in the rear of the boat, playing his accordion. His trousers were rolled up past his knees, and his shoes and good clothes were stuffed into a plastic bag.

He was in his element, singing his favorites as the men joined in, singing and rowing toward the city. A few blocks away, he turned, laughing, and waved to Louise. He would be back later.

These floods came up fast, but they went down the same way. Twenty-four hours, aided by the hot sun, usually left a dry roadbed.

She learned patience—a great deal of patience. When she would forget and become anxious and nervous, her friends would smile and say, "Teacher, your North American is showing."

Louise told a friend that early in their relationship, she and Chon were in a restaurant where a noisy drunk was disturbing the customers. The owner yelled at the man, which did no good. Chon excused himself,

---

[35]   a cold

quietly talked to the man, and led him outside by the arm. Chon was that way. If he had two lempira, he would give one to a beggar. If he had three shirts, he would give one to a friend.

Proud of his third-grade education, he would spend hours trying to write his name with the big flourishes that everyone used. Louise tried to teach him English, but he had little patience and always added an x sound to his words. In a few minutes, he would get frustrated, grab his guitar, and sing back into his world, serenading her as he often did. He lived in his world and didn't want to change a thing.

He would be at the house napping when she came home from school at two or three. A cold plate of fruit would be waiting for her in the refri. Usually, there was a little note at her place at the table where he could show off his fancy writing. Later, when he would leave for work, she would offer him a ride to the city—more precious time together. And it would be sweet.

Mariachi was a brotherhood of musicians. They played singly or in groups, and they would walk the strip from cantinas to restaurants and hotels several times each night, playing and singing. They were clean, groomed, respectful, and Chon was proud to be called Mariachi.

It was strictly a man's world, no women allowed, until the night the fellows needed a ride to a *serenada*. These were special performances contracted by the family, usually for birthdays. Louise picked up the men around 4:15 in the morning, when it was quiet and still, drove to the address, and parked a block from the house to be serenaded.

The *musicos* quietly exited the pickup, careful not to alert the dogs, crept silently up to their spot, and then broke into the traditional *"Feliz Compleaños."*[36] The honoree woke up to music, put on a robe, and the family came to the door.

---

[36]   Happy Birthday

Soon the entire neighborhood was awake and listening, lights came on, and the mariachis sang three or four more folk songs. Everyone sang and clapped and was invited in for coffee. It was a happy time and a traditional way to start a birthday.

Louise stayed in the car. Chon invited her in, but she declined. This was their world, not hers, and she respected that; her presence would bring another world into their tradition. She felt privileged to be able to be a part of this. She chauffeured them to many serenadas and dances in the little aldeas. Good mariachis were respected, and Chon loved his work as one. They often referred to him as Mariachi, much the same as they would refer to her as Teacher.

His *sombrero*[37] was most important to the mariachi, especially a real Western one. They referred to a good one as a *Stetson,* knowing they would probably never own a real one. When she left for the States, she asked Chon what he would like her to bring him.

His answer was quick. "A Stetson."

She swallowed. She knew what they cost.

She almost dreaded the trip. She had always loved flying until September 11. The security blanket was necessary but overwhelming. She missed the good old days. Her biggest fear now was the drug dogs that sniffed the luggage as passengers left the plane in Central America. She even decided to stop taking tea back with her. Probably a silly thing, but anything resembling dried leaves waved a red flag at that time.

A year before—on the morning of September 11, 2001—she had watched the awful news on her television and then driven to the city to Tia Carmen's for a baleada. As she entered, someone kindly turned down the television, and hands reached out to her, lightly touching her arms as she went to her table. It was their way of showing support and love. She was moved.

---

[37]   hat

Now she was noticing the tighter security measures. After arriving in the States, Louise visited her daughter Cindy in Mandan, North Dakota. There she came across a sale of Western hats, something she could afford. She took her own old brown cowboy hat, put it with the new one she had just bought, and tied them up in the authentic Stetson box. What a treat for the fellows who tried to say *Stetson* (accent on the *son;* long *o*) to impress her with their English. She carried the large box with her on the return trip. It just fit into the overhead compartment of the plane. She was pretty pleased with herself.

During her layover in Denver, she had time for a bite, so she set the box on the table and enjoyed her sandwich. She got up and had walked just out of the restaurant when she missed the box. She whirled and ran back.

"Don't touch that. Stop!" a guard yelled.

"It's my hat," she said, and she was at the table with it in her hand.

"Freeze, lady! Stop!" he shouted.

People were backing away. He had his hand on his firearm.

"It's just a hat. Look—" she said, and she slid off the string.

"STOP, LADY! PUT IT DOWN!"

By that time, she had the two hats half out and just stood there.

"They're for my mariachi friend in Honduras. I teach there. Please. What's wrong?"

Then it clicked. 9/11. No boxes. The speakers had all said, over and over, "Don't leave a bag unattended." How foolish she had been.

They came and examined the box, cautiously at first; after that came the lectures.

"Don't you know better than that?"

"What are you doing, carrying that around?"

The guard yelled, the two other security men yelled, everyone yelled. They looked at her like she was a terrorist.

Sheepishly, she took the box and carried it to her gate, to sit and heal. Thinking about it, she must have been flagged and watched from the beginning. It was the box.

Houston, where she overnighted, proved no problem. Then on to Honduras, back to the heat and a new class. She was excited. She was getting older, and her body welcomed the warmth and humidity, which seemed to reach up into the clouds even before they arrived.

The plane landed at San Pedro Sula. As the terminal had not yet been rebuilt after Hurricane Mitch, passengers took the shuttle to the immigration and customs hut. She ran to get a seat.

Boarding, she noticed six or seven Asian-looking men standing toward the front. There was one empty seat directly across from a nice-looking Asian couple. She pushed her way to the seat, which faced the two. The men tried to stop her, but she held her ground and plopped down, the big hatbox safely on her lap. Obviously upset at this, the men spoke to the seated gentleman. He said nothing. The woman smiled at her. The composure and smile indicated *lady*.

"*Buenos tardes*," said Louise. "Isn't this a beautiful day?" she jabbered on in her best Spanish, smiling. "Is this your first visit to Honduras?" she asked.

There was no answer.

The men were standing at her shoulder. Finally, the gentleman signaled with his hand, and they stepped away. They were not happy and kept their eyes on her *and* her big box.

She told the couple she had brought two hats for her mariachi friends. They just smiled and nodded. What she *did* notice was their clothes. Not the run-of-the-mill duds—not at all. These were classy, made from the finest, softest materials. She knew top-notch tailoring when she saw it. These garments had been handmade.

By the time they reached the short distance to the terminal, she was sure she had stepped into the middle of something, and as they pulled to a stop, it was clear. A hand on her shoulder meant "Don't get up yet."

The couple stood, and as they left, Louise said, *"Adios."* The woman smiled and answered quietly. No one else moved. Louise watched them helped off the shuttle then looked out her window. She saw the reception committee, obviously diplomats from Honduras and other countries, including the United States. There were several girls in school uniforms, one carrying a huge bouquet of red roses, which she presented to the *lady.*

Her mind started working. *Oh my goodness.* Her thoughts were verified the next day on the front page of the country's main paper, *La Prensa.* There they were, the same couple, the lovely lady holding the roses and showing the same sweet smile she had given Louise.

As close as she could understand the Spanish caption, she had been sitting across from His Excellency, the prime minister of Taiwan, and his wife.

CHAPTER 8

Dorilla and Paco began to copy Chon's special whistle when he came in the gate. They loved to pretend he was coming. This would get the dogs all excited. Chon's whistle meant he was happy, and Louise would wait to hear that whistle.

If she wasn't downstairs, he would go up and say "Louisà," and they would talk and eat. He was proud of their relationship. I liked the gentle way Chon would say "Louisà" with the soft accent on the *a*, and it became special to me too.

He washed and polished the old pickup every Sunday morning so it would be nice for her to take to church. The cement had to be hosed down each day also, mainly to remove the doggie tracks and the chicken droppings. Chickens . . . well, Louise's lessons were just beginning.

Chon's daughters, Leila and Irma, came to visit their father—Leila from the mountains, and Irma from El Progreso. They had several other sisters and brothers in the mountains. Chon also had another family in a small town south of San Pedro Sula.

Leila was quiet, and Irma, more outgoing. Both were quite lovely. Leila came, bearing a box, and as she was leaving, gave it to Louise, saying, "For your supper."

She repeated it to make sure Louise understood it was *"por su cena."*

Louise nodded and opened the top flap. There, quite contentedly, sat the most beautiful black-and-white hen: a live black-and-white hen.

Chickens had always been one of Louise's fears; their quick pecking frightened her. She caught her breath and said, "How wonderful, but not for *cena*. I will have eggs."

Leila cast a quick glance at Chon, who was obviously proud of his daughter's gift and Louise's happy acceptance. Her look said "What kind of woman is this?"

To Louise, she said, "But you have no *garro*."[38]

The North American schoolteacher threw back her head and laughed—totally ignorant she was treading on very thin ice. "Of course, I can have eggs," she continued. "You don't have to have a rooster to have eggs," she said and tried to explain why.

She not only had insufficient and bad Spanish but had desecrated one of the most cardinal rules of life in Central America: hens cannot live without a rooster. Women cannot survive without men. Who would protect them and tell them what to do? Who would propagate the family and carry on the generations? Their poor father! They were very courteous—feeling, of course, that Chon would set her straight on the ways of life.

Leila and Irma finally said good-bye and left Louise still standing, holding the box with Tessie, as she would henceforth be known.

To Louise's delight, Tessie laid an egg, but Chon, still suffering a prideful blow, was quick to point out it was smaller than it should be, and not of good color; nor was the next one. Finally, Louise, her chicken fears having subsided, decided to get another hen. Chon brought home Big Red and stubbornly announced that neither would do good until they had a garro.

To keep peace, Louise acquiesced and suggested Chon purchase a garro. Home came the happy man, holding the feisty, squawking beast by the feet, a huge smile across his face.

----

[38]   rooster

"Now," he announced, "we will have eggs and chickens."

And they had eggs, same as always, but for Chon, they were perfect. They left some eggs under Tessie and she sat and sat and sat. Louise checked with Carol. Twenty-one days. She waited. *Nothing.* Finally, Chon threw them out.

"Bad eggs," he said.

Chon never knew he had purchased what probably was the only infertile rooster in all of Honduras. Louise quietly borrowed four eggs from a neighbor. Tessie began setting again. She sat and sat, and Louise counted the days.

Early one morning, Chon rushed up the stairs with his hands cupped together, and when he opened them, there was a tiny, fuzzy yellow chick. Louise was ecstatic. She *chicken watched* all day, until four furry yellow chicks were pushing out from Tessie's feathers, sliding down her back, and pecking at her face.

Tessie was a wonderful mother. She would take her little brood to the garden. In Honduras, the yard is referred to as the garden. She would teach them to scratch and get little goodies from the grass and dirt. Sometimes they got in the way of Tessie's foot and went flying, but they scampered back ever so quickly.

At night, they settled under her protective wings and slept. If trouble came or the old rooster started after them, they would scurry under those wonderful wings, and their mom took care of the problem.

Eventually, when they were old enough, Tessie would decide the time had come for them to graduate. No more spending nights under her wings or following her in the grass. She cut it all out totally. It took a few pecks and a little crying, but it was over. Life was different now. They were on their own.

Tessie was Louise's friend. She followed her in the garden, clucked at her, and Louise would talk with her. If Louise was upset or crying,

Tessie sat and looked at her, resting next to her feet. Then came the day Tessie was dragging. A big mass formed on her rear. Chon said it was worms and tried to kill them off with different remedies, but it hurt Tessie. Louise cried.

Chon dug a hole and looked over sadly at Louise. This macho, machete-wielding slayer of beasts and intimidator of women did not have the heart to hurt Tessie.

"You have to, Chon," Louise said.

So he tried. She died hard and was buried, jasmine and ginger flowers decorating her grave. Louise held me and, again, cried in my soft old bear fur.

Big Red was mean as could be, but she and Louise got along. The old rooster disappeared when Louise went to the States. Shortly, there was another home-raised garro in the garden. He was silver and gold and master of his domain—those majestic plumes catching the sunlight in sheer beauty. He would prance in all his glory, his big curved tail feathers moving with the breeze.

He was king, and he knew it. If the hens didn't sit, he got up on the nest and showed them how, then got down and batted them with his wings until they did just what he wanted. Louise often stood and watched, totally transfixed at the life of an animal butchered each day by the thousands.

There was another reason for the chickens: *snakes*. Carol said chickens kept the snake population down. Louise did not like snakes and was ever watchful for them, especially where she lived—on the outskirts of town, with open jungle and fields in back.

Most feared was the barba amarilla, an aggressive viper, extremely poisonous and fatal. People said if you could get to a curandero[39] he could possibly save you. But with a twenty-to-thirty-minute window, the possibility was remote.

---

[39]   black healer

Running a close second and found twice in her house and garden was the coral snake—some with the yellow band and some without, all with a horrid little blunt nose in front of poison-filled glands. If Louise looked out and saw the chickens jumping up and down, pecking at something, she knew it must be some poor snake that was where it shouldn't be, and she would smile.

One unseasonably hot afternoon, Louise came home from school very tired. Chon wasn't back yet, so she went past me, reaching out to touch my furry head as she often did, and then on up the stairs. She took off her blouse and trousers. There was sweat running off her back in tiny trickles. A little breeze started making its way through the big windows.

She sat down in the corner of the old brown love seat, watched television for about thirty minutes, and then got up to dress. Something heavy was pulling down on the left side of her panties. She looked down.

It was big, about the size of a huge orange, black as coal, and furry. She knew, of course, it was a tarantula. A big one. I saw her raise her hand and then flip it back hard, knocking the spider to the floor. It scampered to the closest dark spot, up under the sofa table.

She ran down to the kitchen, grabbed the Raid and a wide-mouthed bottle. The spray slowed it enough to put in the bottle. She set it up on the stairway to wait for Chon and got dressed.

She heard him whistle and smiled smugly, eager to show him what she had captured. When he didn't come up, she called, "Chon!"

The sound of metal hitting the floor rang out. "Chon, be careful of the tiles. Don't hit them!"

One word, "*culebra*,"[40] was the answer.

"Oh, dear God."

---

[40]   snake

She ran down the stairs. It was hiding behind the little apartment-sized stove.

"Louisà, if you tip the stove out, I can get him."

She looked unbelievingly at Chon. Finally, gritting her teeth, she held on to the stove and tipped it out toward her. Chon quickly killed the snake. He was powerful, skilled with the machete, raised in the mountains, and knew all about those things. He took out the weapon with a long greenish snake draped across it. A few spasms from the animal brought more shudders from Louise.

When Chon came back into the house after tossing the snake over the fence, Louise was sitting on the stairs, pointing to the jar with the tarantula.

"Chon," she said, "please get my suitcase. I'm going home."

From my vantage point in the corner, I saw his frantic reaction and some true Latin *amor* come forth. He talked to her, caressed her, cajoled her, begged her, and she stayed. But there was a rubber piece put at the bottom of all the doors. No more unwanted guests.

Louise had an outside cage for the birds, a large one, with wooden branches to climb and gnaw on—everything a parrot could want. The racket that came from the cage one Sunday afternoon sent her running out.

Standing up close, she looked all over the inside for a snake, or *picheti*. Nothing. The birds quieted. She stepped back and looked down.

There, by her ankle, winding its way down the metal leg of the cage was a most vivid red-and-black snake. She simply stopped and watched it. The red was vibrant, luminous.

Hypnotized for just a moment, she grasped hold of her thoughts and ran for the machete. The dogs had already sniffed it out, and she was afraid for them. She slapped at each of them with the broad side of the machete to move them back.

The red and black bands were hurrying through the grass. She raised the machete and brought it down. Two pieces of snake scurried in opposite directions. She hit it again. She couldn't decide which part was the head. Then she brought down the machete once more. Chon said the tail had a barb that could inject poison too. She had passed it off as a mountain myth, but now she wasn't sure. So she took another slice at it. Finally, there was no movement from any of the many pieces.

She gave the dogs another swat, ran for a pail and the shovel, and scooped all the little red and black pieces into the pail. She wondered what she should do with them, then took two clothespins and pinned the handle of the pail to the clothesline. Chon would know.

She heard his whistle, welcomed him, and asked him to do something with the pail on the line. He took it down, looked in it, glanced up at her through the window, walked to the edge of the garden, and emptied it over the fence.

His only words coming back into the kitchen were *"Es muy peligrosa."*[41]

She said, *"Si."*

He looked at her again and motioned for her to go out. Then he took the machete and said, *"Escuchame."*[42] And he proceeded to explain: "Never kill a snake with the sharp side, Louisà. You will have two snakes to chase, and you could get bitten. Always use the dull side. Hit it hard. You will break its back, and it can't move."

She shuddered, but listened intently.

Louise always said she couldn't understand why God made snakes—that He must have really had a bad day!

---

[41]   It is very dangerous.

[42]   Listen to me.

CHAPTER 9

Many times I saw Louise go out on the balcony depressed, homesick, lonely, and usually in tears.

She would talk out loud, "Why, God? Why am I still here? What more? I've taught. I've helped. What more is it I am supposed to do? Maybe it's time I pack up and go home where I belong."

It never happened. I heard her so torn, like some force was holding her back. Something always came up—a teacher would leave or get sick, maybe even die, and she would be asked to take another class. Always something. So family and home again got shoved to the back burner, until the next year.

And then there was this little girl.

Crista was the younger sister of one of Louise's earlier students. She knew the parents well. Isa and Giovanni ran a restaurant and hotel on the beach, a very nice one where she loved to go, relax, and watch the ocean. On a hot day, it was like an oasis, the warm shade with the gentle ocean breeze moving the big palm fronds, the sound of the waves softly breaking on the white sand, creating an atmosphere like those in the paradise brochures.

The third-grade teacher left, and the school asked Louise to take over the class. She agonized over this. The year before, she had covered a few classes in second grade, and the professor told her, "Don't worry about Crista. She doesn't learn, and she won't answer you. Just ignore her."

The child sat quietly at her desk, slumped over, a tall fawn-like little girl with big brown eyes and long dark brown hair. She never spoke; neither did she take part in classwork.

Louise knew that if she took third grade, she would have to talk with the parents and explain that Crista should possibly not continue her schooling there. She also knew this would absolutely not be acceptable to them, and being rather affluent, they were important financially to the school. She was caught in a touchy situation.

Crista was enrolled in third grade. Lineup was at seven o'clock, in the outside court, with all classes present. The country's national anthem was sung and the pledge was said, followed by announcements for the day and often a program. Crista always came late, quietly slipped into line, and later slumped in her seat, head down, her hair falling around her face. She did not participate.

She brought a poster to school one day, doubtless prompted by her mother, but it was a beginning. Isa was a good mother, and Louise's heart went out to her. Crista's poster was hung on the wall of the classroom. She was proud.

Louise loved spelling and made it one of her most important classes. Friday was test day. She would entice the children with stickers of their favorite cartoon characters, and if they all had 95 percent or higher, there was ice cream for everyone.

The test consisted of twenty words, and Crista always got the first three or four. Then she would get nervous, flustered, and could not concentrate well enough to finish. She was having a terrible time one day. "It's all right, Crista," Louise said. "Just get what you can, and I will give you the others at recess."

At recess she was there and took the words. One word, *musician*, was written down quickly and correctly. Obviously, learning was not Crista's problem. Getting it out and down on paper was where she floundered. As weeks went on, she perked up a little. She still caught up at recess, and there was always praise for her work. As she progressed, she began coming to school on time and paid attention. Her head was held higher, and she laughed and talked with the others.

It was a special day when Crista finished her exam with the class, a proud smile across her face, even though she missed two.

The next week the class was almost electric with anticipation for the exam. It began, the words dictated slowly and distinctly, all eyes zeroed in on Teacher, concentration at its keenest. Everyone finished, including Crista.

Papers were collected, and although they were told to stay back, they packed around Teacher's desk, all sixteen boys and four girls. Exams were checked; nineteen papers were each marked with 95 percent or 100 percent and awarded a sticker. Finally, the last one—Crista's.

There was a hush in the room. Teacher went down the words. Crista's classmates, aware of her struggle, had never complained at the extra help during recess.

The last word on Crista's paper was checked, and as a big red 100 percent was marked at the top, a huge cheer rocked the room. She glowed. Her mother was waiting in the salon for the news.

As school closed that afternoon and Louise was getting ready to leave, Isa stepped into the room. She had tears in her eyes and put her arms around Teacher. "Thank you, Louisà," she said over and over. They talked often after that, laughing at how Crista made her two brothers work on their homework and how diligent she had become.

At the end of her sixth and final elementary year, an election was held for King, Queen, Prince, and Princess of Holy Spirit Episcopal Bilingual School. Crista was a Princess.

Teacher stood with the crowd as the royals paraded down the avenue. Crista walked alone, tall, straight as a willow, head held high, a proud smile endearing her to everyone along the way. Her hair was pulled back and clipped loosely at the back of her neck with a gold clasp, then fell straight down to her waist.

She wore a gold-bronze long gown—simple, elegant. Her big brown doe eyes were happy, and she walked with a confident, easy grace, waving to everyone.

There was a huge lump in Louise's throat. *All right, God. Thank you.*

And now she knew. She knew that if for nothing else, her years there had helped one child find her place.

CHAPTER 10

Louise never missed school. Those little ones were so important to her. She was at the gate at six in the morning, and by seven, she was ready to face the class. It was already hot, and beads of perspiration dripped off her chin and trickled down her back. Everyone carried little towels or washcloths to wipe the sweat from their faces, but she really didn't mind it. For some reason, her body felt so much better in the heat.

She taught second, third, fourth, fifth—wherever they needed her. I retired many times, only to be called back for some reason or other. I sat there, so quiet in my corner, and watched her work late, night after night, and often, weekends.

Chon would say, "Louisà, you work too hard." He always pitched in and did the wash and the cooking, especially when she was working on Saturdays, Sundays, and holidays. He was a good cook. When she was making window scenes, camels for Navidad, whales, or a seven-foot Goliath for a church program, Chon would always help cut those huge pieces of cardboard.

After long hours of work he would bring coffee upstairs, and they would rest out on the balcony in the gentle breeze, watch the hummingbirds, and look at the orchids and flowers. She loved the orchids, which grew wild there in the tropics, and had dozens of plants up on the balcony. Tree bark is extremely hard to cut, so Chon always helped her put her orchids on the bark, to hang on the corner posts and walls.

I witnessed so much those years—the many hours sewing dresses for folk dances, suits for the boys to wear under the camels, and making paper-mache planets for her class. There was a gigantic bull's head of paper-mache, a life-size Canadian Mountie for international studies, and full-sized figures of the Nativity dressed in clothes of real material. The Nativity was for her class's window.

Protected by metal bars, the huge window, which extended most of the way across the side of the room, was a perfect place to attach cardboard scenes. Situated in the center of the school, it was visible to all, and first to greet visitors.

During the time the Nativity scene covered the window, niños in the first and second grades would reach up and touch Mary's blue robes or the straw in the manger. It filled them with wonder and made a connection. Louise and her class would watch quietly behind the window and smile at each other.

Discipline in her classes was important. Latin children, especially the boys, were pampered, often to the point of spoiling, and that didn't work in Louise's classes.

In Honduras, schoolchildren can never be disciplined by grabbing an arm, swatting, slapping, or through verbal abuse, such as sharp words or raised voices. The extreme heat, fatigue, and frustration could cause teachers to slip. If one should lose his temper and commit any of these infractions, he would immediately be arrested, along with the director, and imprisoned until such time a judge could hear the case.

Carol saw a fifth-grade boy fondling a young girl. She made a sharp, shaming comment to the boy. Ten minutes after school had been dismissed, the police arrived and took Carol and the director into custody.

Carol's children came to Louise for help. Thankfully, the judge heard the case that evening. All Louise could do was to give Carol a ride home. She never asked what happened, and Carol never volunteered any information. In the third world, one knows not to say or know too much.

Louise walked the fine line. She got terribly frustrated but demanded a great deal from her niños. By pushing and keeping their interest peaked, she managed to get the discipline—at the same time instilling the math, reading, spelling, science, calligraphy, and grammar, which they hated with a passion.

She told her classes, "You are good. I am proud of each of you. One day, when I am back up in the United States, I will pick up a newspaper and see one of your names there, announcing to the world that you are either the president or in the cabinet of the Honduran government. This is your country, and you must prepare yourself to step up and lead."

Then she would smile and say, "And that is why you have to learn your grammar." She firmly believed what she said. Her students were that good, and she was proud of each of them.

Discipline was also a big factor in her programs—teaching folk dances she knew nothing about or training sixteen wonderfully uncoordinated third-grade boys and four girls how to do a dance made of exercise moves. This line dance, as she later learned it was called, was a huge success for the Father's Day program, with each of the niños dressed in his father's T-shirt, necktie, and one of his baseball caps.

They studied hard. She demanded much, and they gave it. Then they played, equally hard. One of the favorites was a trip to the beach, usually to fly kites. During art class, she had tried to teach them how to make a kite according to the book. They smiled.

Josè Manuel raised his hand. He was a leader, happy, always seeming to quietly anticipate her needs; he was very special to her.

"With respect, Mrs. Langford," Josè Manuel said, "could we teach you how we make kites?"

Surprised, she said, "Yes, of course."

They stripped the green from the main veins of the thin palm leaves, strong but very light, tied three stems together using plain sewing thread, wove it around the outside, covered the frames with china[43] paper, and added tails. The kites were ready to fly, with only sewing thread for string, and were almost weightless.

She was sure they wouldn't go up, but off the class went, each one excitedly carrying their masterpiece the two blocks to the beach. They ran with the kites in the ocean breeze, and every one sailed up. It was glorious and unbelievable. Those bright colors flew, dancing and bobbing in the breeze, way up—on sewing thread. They flew so high the helicopters patrolling the beach on drug patrol turned out of their way to miss them. People gathered to watch, and parents were eager to help.

Each class, every year, made kites. She kept china paper in her home for the children of the barrio. They would come rattle her gate to get their three pieces of paper, and the skies would be filled with color.

The most disciplined, however, was a class with sixteen girls and four boys, which was a complete reverse from the year before. She trained them in a precision drill—marching singly, breaking into doubles, then four across, crisscrossing without a moment's hesitation and working flags Chon had helped her make, red satin on one side and white on the other.

She dressed them in short red circle skirts and a plain, loose sleeveless top. Their hair was up in a bun, mothers had applied the makeup, and they wore little white canvas shoes. Before the girls went out, they were scared, giggling nervously. "Mrs. Langford, I have to go to the bathroom."

"Hurry."

Then she looked at them.

"Okay. Pull yourselves up. You are good. *So good.* I want you to pretend you are Britney Spears [their idol]. Think, 'I am Britney Spears, and

---

43   tissue

this is my audience. I am going to go out, smile, make them love me, and show them what I can do.'" She saw the smiles come to their faces.

The music started. They strutted out. Louise held her breath. It was a stiff routine, and she hoped it would be half as good as they had practiced. The leader, Julissa, marched, her back ramrod straight. She blew her whistle; bodies turned as one.

The two lines, led by Carmen and Vanessa, crisscrossed and twirled their flags without flaw. They marched, turned, smiled, broke into doubles, then fours, formed lines back and forth, never wavering. They were sure of themselves and held their heads high. *They did it.* Then it was over.

For just a second, there was dead silence. Mothers and fathers couldn't believe what they had seen. Programs before had been the wiggly-hipped *punta* dances with the sexy costumes the Latins loved. This was totally new.

A thunderous applause broke the silence. There were whistles and screams. People stood and clapped. One mother commented, "I can't believe what I just saw. Danielle can't even tie her own shoes in the morning." Louise loved it.

A year later, this same class, with the exception of six students, all failed their grade. The director called Louise to the office. "Mrs. Langford, we have to do something," she said. "Is it possible for you to work with these students for one week and I will examine them again?"

Louise cringed. She knew the students. They were a little lazy, but she had good work out of them. She also knew their teacher. He was Jamaican, and although he spoke the King's English, as he put it, even Louise couldn't understand him.

She went to work, laid it on the line for the kids and the parents, and they began. Taking their teacher's college grammar terms, she broke them down into phrases the students could understand. She drilled them, practiced with them, talked, lectured, explained, and then drilled some more.

They were exhausted. So was she.

Exam day came. Their new grade would be averaged with the old, so they had to do extremely well to pass.

Students finished and gathered out by the gate, where the parents were standing in groups, waiting. Some of the niños were crying, others worriedly clinging to their moms and dads—all very serious.

Louise corrected the papers in her classroom, alone, elated at what she was seeing. The director stepped into the room and they talked. The woman closed the conversation by saying, "Thank you, Mrs. Langford. I will think this over."

As Louise went out the gate, the parents surged forward. "Please, Miss, we are taking the children to the pool and lunch at the beach. We would like you to be our guest." She couldn't refuse, but she knew what they wanted.

When they finished eating, everyone quieted down, all eyes on her. Finally, she said, "I thank you for the lovely meal. You know I can't tell you the grades. I am bound by the rules. Please don't ask. I *can* say I was very pleased at the work I saw." That was how it had to be.

The next day, grades were posted. All passed on to the fifth grade; two were on probation.

She retired in 2007 and, during the summer, went back to the States for hip surgery. She returned in the fall. A phone call early one morning asked permission for the school's director and bookkeeper to visit her. She welcomed Mrs. Barrera and Farida. Hondurans never go right to the point; there are always the respectful amenities. She was fine, she answered, and glad to be back. Then it was time for the business at hand.

"Mrs. Langford, we lost our history teacher this morning. He was taken to the hospital yesterday and died early today. We would like you to take his classes, if you could."

"Of course," she found herself saying. "I would be glad to. I will get ready and come to the school." She couldn't believe she had agreed, but secretly, she felt good. She had been lost without the school, the children, and her fellow teachers.

She was in the class by lunch break. It had been many years since she studied history. She was now faced with US History, geography, and world history. For the first time, she was working with older students. They were a challenge, especially the discussions.

In 2008, the United States had presidential elections. It was surprising how interested this little Central American country was in US politics. The senior class began debating the Clinton-Obama race, girls versus guys. Discussions were active and interesting. Often a hand would go up, asking her questions she dared not answer.

"Mrs. Langford, why is my country like it is? Why do we have problems?"

Many times, the word *corruption* quietly came into the question.

Louise was careful yet honest. These were good students, smart, and looking for answers. But she knew every word would go back home and out through the city. Her answer was, "You have a wonderful country. You are simply having growing pains. Every country has them, even the US. You should be proud of your country."

They smiled and looked at her. "Really, Mrs. Langford? You are the first teacher that has said something nice about our country."

After the US primaries were over, they began debating the issues of the election. Interest was intense. When Louise received her absentee ballot, she took it to school to show the classes.

"Fill it out, Mrs. Langford."

"Oh no. That is something I do in private."

"Please, we want to see how you vote."

"No, that is my right. No one sees my ballot."

And later, "Mrs. Langford, tell us who you voted for."

She just smiled. It was like her age. That was her business, just hers.

Discussions became very sensitive.

"He can't win," they said. "He's not white." Then they would steal a quick look for her reaction.

"It can happen," said Louise. "Anyone can be president. You can be anything you want to."

"No way."

"Well, we'll wait and see how it goes."

Election night, as she drove down the dusty road at sunset, past the rows of little cement houses to her two-story home at the end of the street, she noticed every television was on, volume up. Everyone was watching CNN Español or CNN English for the US election returns. There was no one in the street, no distractions—just the election. She was surprised.

She chained the dogs, put the pickup inside, let the dogs loose, and went up to watch the returns herself.

At nine thirty, just as CNN was calling Obama's election, she heard voices outside, under her balcony in the front.

Stepping out, she saw close to twenty-five smiling faces looking up from the street.

"Teacher, did you know you have a new president? Isn't that wonderful? It's Mr. Obama."

"Yes, it is. Thank you." And she waved at them and went back in.

They all knew they had seen history made that night. When she saw the president-elect walk out on that huge platform alone, she too knew it was a moment to remember.

The next day, she parked her car across from the school, passed through the gate, and stepped into the schoolyard.

"Mrs. Langford! He did it," Darrel shouted from back by the school. He was tall, at least six feet three inches, and a superb athlete. He came running, picked her up, and swung her around.

"You were right. I can do anything I want. I really can. This proves it. You were right!"

Many times, she reached for paper and pen to write to the new president-elect, telling him of the hope he had brought to so many people. She could not believe the reaction in this little Central American country. Pictures of the new president and his family covered the two major papers and the television, their every move captured and shown. It was a great moment for many oppressed people.

CHAPTER 11

Cultures are an interesting thing. If one culture believes the same as another, they are good. If their belief takes a different direction or path, they are labeled heathen, sinner, criticized, and efforts are made to try to change their thinking. Some part of this may be well and good, but for many, it is solely the power-hungry flexing their muscles.

Most missionaries were wonderful people, helpful and self-sacrificing. Others had a great deal of "I" trouble. Louise became very cautious around them. She did not flaunt the fact that she was a missionary. Instead, she quietly tried to help and support where she could. Praying was good and necessary, but the extent to which some took it and the display they made of it certainly did not impress her.

Louise believed in a hands-on ministry and talked to God constantly and mentally, as she told all her classes. When she felt the need for time away, she would go to her house or garden, the ocean, or walk in a quiet street. God was everywhere; however, she could concentrate on listening to him better in private.

She watched pious, almost arrogant, self-satisfied people come to this poor country to save souls, condemning their beliefs and holding themselves on a plane above the gentle folk. She often wondered what Jesus would have said, and then she felt guilty; she had been judging them herself, which was wrong.

Religion and faith began taking on a different meaning for her.

School was her first priority, but she found another passion, another way to help the children.

The mountains were set across the main highway, rising steeply into jungle and a silent world that sent its own "no trespassing" warning. She and Jean Valentine would pick up a few bomberos at the police station and go to the mountains to check on niños who needed to see doctors coming with the brigade.

Jean was a nurse. She was born and raised in Honduras and had later gone to the States. She came back to her homeland to help the children— *her children*, as she called them—and did it with fervor. She worked the media, radio and television, and was a constant visitor at city hall.

She ramrodded a home for the aged and an SOS refuge for children— whether orphaned, abandoned, abused, or in trouble. Fund-raisers were organized, and rights were demanded for *her people*. She was a force to reckon with, a good and powerful woman who carried the respect of the entire city, and she was Louise's friend.

It was Jean who introduced Louise to the medical brigades, and she eagerly volunteered her weekends to help. From that first year, when Louise had visited Josè Manuel in the hospital, she was astounded at the lack of medical facilities. What they did have was outdated or in need of repair. The staff worked tirelessly with what they had, but they lacked almost everything. Noticing there were no cribs, she talked to a carpenter friend, and two weeks later, a horse and cart delivered three white cribs to the hospital. She was ready to get involved.

Her first brigade was with a large international group and had an emotional impact on her she had not expected. Arriving early to be ahead of the crowd, she was astounded to find literally hundreds of people standing, waiting in the hot sun to try to get a number to see a doctor. Many brought umbrellas, and it looked like a field of colorful flowers. They made way for her to get in the gate, hands reaching out to try to get her attention, asking her to help them.

It was heartbreaking when all but 250 had to be turned away. She also found forcing religious ideas on those needing medical attention quite distasteful to her. Before people were given medicine, they were lectured on being saved. She noticed Jean, tight-lipped, quiet, and knew she was not alone in her displeasure at what was happening.

She quickly decided to disassociate herself from that group and work the brigades Jean brought in twice a year—each with an internist, a plastic surgeon, an orthopedic surgeon, and a gynecologist. When the brigades came, Jean's group met them at the airport, fed and housed them, ran the triage, the surgeries, and finally took them back to the airport. These doctors and nurses had to bring everything with them— the drugs, the instruments, and all the needed supplies in black suitcase after black suitcase.

Jean's brigades were for children only, and no child was ever turned away. This was where Louise's help was needed. Two hundred people usually came from the city, mountains, farms, or outskirts, and gathered in the hot sun to keep their place in line for treatment.

Triage was held at the hospital. Louise's job was to organize the sick and crippled patients into lines, youngest and smallest first. She had to log absolutely everything—name, family, age, nature of the illness, etc. Hondurans were famous for their bookwork, especially when it involved their children.

Sometimes, approaching a soft-spoken young woman holding a bundle, Louise would ask, "*Que problema?*"[44] Her heart sank as the mother uncovered a beautiful baby, so perfect, down to the open hole under the nose. The blanket was always replaced quickly. These children were never taken out with others. Theirs was a hard life, and there were so many.

After three brigades, one young doctor brought some medical friends from the States and taught the doctors in La Ceiba how to perform the plastic surgery required for these cleft palates. Louise had seen his face during that first triage with her group. He could not mask his utter

---

[44]   What is the problem?

disbelief at the injuries, disfigurements, and diseases that were so quietly being brought before him.

Days in the brigade were long and hot. Louise always tried to carry extra water. No one in line would ask, but their eyes talked. She would pass out all she had, and they shared. The heat was intense, and sometimes they could rig a canopy over the lines of waiting families.

Triage was in a large square room with four tables, one for each doctor. Crowded and hot, it was made more bearable by a big white metal fan, which stirred the air enough for a little breeze. A string across one corner held a white sheet for a bit of privacy during examinations. Older students were brought in from schools to translate for the doctors.

After the first day, the hospital allowed the doctors to take over the operating room for three to four days. They worked long hours, especially hard when they weren't accustomed to the heat.

Many children were sent, all expenses paid, to the United States for surgery and treatment—or on to other doctors in Honduras. Doctors and hospitals in the States donated their services. The airlines were always able to find seats for the children and their escorts at no expense.

It was hard to send a child for help. Parents did not want to let their children out of their sight, especially with the child-trafficking problems in the Latin countries. Paperwork for the government was unending, and along with being expensive, groups had to be contacted to transport these children. Casa Corazòn stepped up to help with that problem.

Organizing and putting on a brigade was a gigantic task for Jean and her group. Louise would drag home late in the afternoon to her quiet green garden, some cold water, and a plate of fruit Chon had left in the refri. She needed to rest and prepare for school the next day.

Jean's group was ATAN, a Spanish-titled organization meaning "Telenos Helping Children." Always looking for ways to raise money for their brigades, it was a good day when Louise met some visitors from

California. She managed to get a huge donation from a most wonderful lady and her hostel group.

Some of this money provided hearing aids for twenty-seven children who had been totally deaf all their lives. It was hard not to become emotional when there were tears from a young man hearing his mother's voice for the first time, the wonder of a little boy listening to a bird, and the hands over the ears at the traffic from outside. Louise was proud to be part of this group.

Between the teaching and the brigades, there wasn't much time for life. Bedtime came early, and morning, earlier. But it was fulfilling and rewarding.

Until the day she left, I watched Louise put on her turquoise jacket and leave for big Children's Day celebrations or a brigade. It seemed she was always on the go, but a few hours in that hot sun really sapped her strength.

Many things happened at our house. Oftentimes, on Friday, the teachers would come after school. They brought food, rolled back the carpet, shoved the furniture over, and danced. They loved to dance, the music getting louder and louder. Hondurans love loud music and usually turned it on full volume, like the air conditioners—all the way on or all the way off. They couldn't seem to understand *comfortable*.

She was happy to have the teachers come. Her yard was beautiful, with its flowering bushes, every color imaginable: huge bougainvillea, hibiscus, jasmine, poinsettias, and many others she couldn't name. They seemed to grow overnight.

The country was like a greenhouse, humid and hot. She even had chili plants, the hot little red ones. Latinos liked their chilies, and restaurants usually had a jar of these sitting on the table. Louise was warned, "Don't take a bite until you try a tiny drop." She barely touched her mouth with the juice; her tongue was on fire. She found it hard to believe people could eat them. She also found she had to be careful not to touch her face when picking them; it would burn. Her neighbors all liked them; there was no problem giving away what Chon didn't use.

She loved growing things and had beautiful princess palms both in front and back of her home. A mango tree had sprouted from a seed tossed by a worker and grew higher than the house.

She got along well with her neighbors, until it came to the loud music. Her house was up high, and she heard every bass note. It reverberated all the way through her and drove her crazy. She didn't cope well with that at all. This was Chon's world; he never understood how it bothered her.

During Navidad she sat on the back balcony to get away from the loud music and exploding firecrackers. She hated firecrackers! I heard her say, "How can they be so hungry and in need and still find enough money to buy firecrackers?"

Cuetas[45] began early Christmas Eve. By midnight, there were big ones, blasting in all directions. The dogs ran to hide from the sound; it was so loud it shook my stuffing. It was their culture. They loved their firecrackers and their loud music.

---

[45]   firecrackers

CHAPTER 12

Louise's friend, Jean, once laughed and said, "I think one of the main topics among the heavenly host is *Who is on Louise duty today?*"

Driving in the third world is dangerous. When she bought her pickup, insurance was nonexistent. In an injury accident, the driver at fault usually went to prison, unless he could afford compensation for all kinds of involved persons. North Americans were especially vulnerable. To a poor native, the risk of injury, even injury itself, was small compared to compensation from a rich northerner.

Usually in smaller accidents, the one who could yell the loudest and talk the fastest won. Officials were seldom called. If a taxi was involved, there were many fellow taxistas who witnessed the accident. She tried to be very careful.

Louise's first car accident happened the Friday before Mother's Day. It was noon, and she was headed back to school for the Mother's Day program. As she was going up the main street to the highway, something banged into the right front side of her pickup. She slid to a stop in the middle of the street and jumped out to check. People had stopped walking and were looking. No one moved to help.

A man was getting up from the ground. When he saw Louise, he quickly grabbed the opportunity and began to hold his arm. His bike, a new one with wrappers still on the handlebars, was crumpled behind her front tire.

"She hit me! She hit me!" he yelled to the crowds on the sidewalk, but no one said anything or moved.

Surely, someone saw him run into me, she thought. She looked frantically at the faces for help. They were all totally blank. *Nothing.* The road was blocked, and cars were honking. Buses were piling up, more honking, the buses blasting the air with their loud horns. At that moment, a pickup loaded with police stopped, and officers bailed out of the back.

She tried to talk to them. Her Spanish was so bad. She used her hands, shook her head. They never even saw her. She was a woman. She didn't exist. She was frustrated and getting upset, which did her absolutely no good.

They talked with the man. Blackie was his name. Evidently, he was delivering a new bike. She was sure she was going to prison. No one would listen. The sun was ungodly hot. The honking was becoming intolerable. They examined the bike and shook their heads. *Dear God,* she thought.

Then Blackie made a big mistake. He had been drinking and took a swing at one of the policemen. Quicker than she could blink, they grabbed him, threw him in the police pickup, threw the bike in with him, climbed in, and left. She didn't know what to do.

Standing there in her dress uniform in front of her pickup, horns blasting unmercifully from every direction, she looked helplessly at the crowds on the sidewalk. Everyone was looking at her, their hands moving to the right, urging her to "go, go, go." She climbed into the pickup and went, looking back constantly to see if the police were chasing her.

As she drove up to the school, two teachers ran to meet her. "Are you okay?"

"Yes," she said.

"Someone called the school. We were ready to come try to get you out of prison. This can be serious, Mrs. Langford."

She knew.

School functions ate up so much of her time. Programs, one after the other, lesson plans, meetings, dinners, and graduations all took preparation. A welcome respite came in the spring: *Semana Santa*.[46] No school for the entire week.

Semana Santa marked the beginning of the last part of the school year for the bilingual schools and full swing into the final preparations for big events, culminating with three graduations: kinder, sixth, and the *instituto*.

This was the week when thousands upon thousands flocked to the beach at Tela to stake their claim on enough space in the sand to live for two to three days.

Semana Santa—when families were together and the world was a wonderful place. No one cared what you had on, or what you were doing. Brand-name swimsuits splashed in the churning ocean next to naked bodies. Everyone was happy.

Louise tried never to go to the city that week. It was zero tolerance with the police—no questions, just off to prison. There were plenty of ladrones. She learned not to wear anything she didn't want stolen.

Buses carried approximately one hundred people each, packed four to a seat and standing. Lined up along the highway above Tela for miles, these buses dumped up to ten thousand happy vacationers on the little town for a week of swimming, eating, sleeping, and drinking.

Multitudes from these transports walked down the road to town filling the entire street, carrying bottles, baskets, coolers, towels, babies, blankets—everything imaginable. Smiles were on every face, their eyes focused solely on the beach at the end of the street. Bathrooms were at a premium, the *policia* and *transitos* were out in force, and businesses flourished, especially the Coca-Cola, Pepsi, and Salva Vida and Port Royal beer companies.

---

[46]   Holy Week

From the beginning, people's lives seem geared toward a certain point—the lessons, teachings, contacts and interests, all building toward a goal. For Louise, that seemed to be the work in Honduras. Everything she had done equipped her more fully for the tasks there. It was as if fate stepped in. The blueprints were on the table, and with God as her guide, she slipped into the future there.

Starting with her first look at those twenty-two little faces and thinking, *Oh, God, I'll never tell them apart,* to receiving the parents' award for her part in forming their children's futures. From driving the mountain trails to directing pageants for special occasions, these events called upon her talents to their fullest.

Holy Spirit was famous for their programs. There was one for every occasion—Mother's Day, Father's Day, Christmas, Day of Grace, Easter, Day of the Child, etc. There was at least one each month, and Louise worked hard to put on good programs. This was fine, except, with each good one, they would expect more in the future.

Families and friends flocked to these presentations and often talked and visited all the way through. It was a challenge for the teachers, and sometimes all the work went unheard. Louise made sure hers were different. She found success in quick action, no talk, cute dance steps, and beautiful costumes.

One of her favorites was a folk dance she reworked to accommodate her smallest class of eight girls and four boys. The sewing machine went into overtime. Dresses, one of every color of the rainbow, with double-circled, tiered skirts, and laden with yards and yards of rickrack, spewed out from under the needle. She made two pairs of black trousers for the boys inside the bull and designed a black cape to create the back, which was attached to a huge wire-based paper-mache head. Two boys, bending over beneath the cape, brought the bull to life. The other two boys were dressed as matadors.

The bull came in from the back of the church. Hundreds of people who had come to the Mother's Day program screamed, grabbed their babies, and moved to the walls. The boys in the bull seized the moment. They charged the two little matadors, teasing them, stomped at the audience, and finally broke into a dance, kicking their feet out to the side in rhythm, obviously enjoying every moment.

Seconds later, the girls—each in a different colored dress, their hair woven into a long black braid, and a flower over their right ear—danced in from the sides of the stage. Latinos are so emotionally charged. The mothers screamed and cried at how beautiful their daughters were; camera-toting dads jockeyed for a spot to take pictures, and the girls knew they owned the show. They threw back their shoulders and danced their hearts out. It was a glorious success. Cheers and tears!

Another favorite was something she had always dreamed of—the total Navidad presentation. She wrote the script in Spanish and used the entire student body, all 220.

The set, designed by the art department, came from many sections of six-foot-tall cardboard panels placed one next to the other across the entire stage. The front of the church had become the city of Bethlehem, complete with doors for the innkeepers, and the stable with its animals and the waiting manger.

At the beginning, the burro (played by the same two boys as the bull and made similarly) came in carrying a very small Mary. She rode all the way from the back of that long church to the front as Joseph walked at her side, past Roman soldiers and a census taker. It was so basic and beautiful. People responded with the usual tears, and as Joseph carefully reached up and gently lifted Mary down, the women patted their husbands' arms and nodded their heads.

Emotions were at an all-time high. When Joseph finally got Mary nestled in the stable, all the little angels came forth, the air ringing with their sweet songs.

Then, from every doorway and back room came the shepherds, conversing with each other loudly so people could hear, and pointing to the big bright star sailing across the heavens. This put the audience right in the middle of the action, which is exactly how Louise had planned it.

Finally, the pièce d' résistance! She had studied pictures of the Egyptians and Romans carrying people in chairs, sitting on a frame that fit over the slaves' shoulders. *Why not?* she thought. *Of course.* Her neighbor was a blacksmith. He looked at her with disbelief, but yes, he would make her three frames to rest on the men's shoulders. Each would have two humps for the carriers' heads, thus making a perfect space between for the wise men to sit.

It looked good on paper, and it worked. The camels' heads were life-sized and cut of dark heavy cardboard and then attached to the body frame, which had been covered with camel-tan cloth. High school boys underneath each wore camel-tan trousers and socks to match.

Reins of beads, gold fringes, and tassels decorated the camels' heads, and the three wise men threw fancy gold, silver, and bright-colored scarves on the camels' backs to sit on.

As the children finished singing and the shepherds were kneeling, the announcer began, "And it came to pass, there were three wise men . . ."

The back doors opened, and the three camels slowly walked in, the wise men sitting up in their seats on the camels' backs, discussing what they had brought for the new king.

Pandemonium broke as people stood, moved to the walls, and clapped. As the camels reached the front, they carefully kneeled. The wise men dismounted without incident, and again, cheers, tears, and applause as all the students broke into a resounding "Gloria." The cameraman caught the entire production, and it was shown on the local television station each day until Christmas.

Louise was so fatigued that when Dr. Carlos grabbed her and hugged her, she almost collapsed. She was so tired she hurt. She could hardly put one foot in front of the other until she could get home—just get home and rest.

A few days before Navidad, Continental Airlines contacted Jean and the ATAN group. Each year, they took toys to some areas of the countries they serviced. That year they would be in Tela. The director of the airlines came with his family and boxes of toys.

Jean had picked an area called Grant, a little barrio on the outskirts of town. Because of the rain, the group couldn't get up the mountain, so they sent word for the people to walk down. And they came—more than two hundred children under twelve years of age, followed by many older ones. There were clean ones, dirty ones, some dressed up, many in rags, mothers carrying babies, laughing children, and crying children. They were like ants swarming down the road. The director and his family stood mesmerized. It was unbelievable.

There were dolls for the girls and trucks for the boys. Jean had taken three extra bomberos as the area was a pretty dangerous one, and it took them all to keep order so everyone could get a gift.

Soon, it was over and they were saying good-bye to the director. Louise noticed a man starting up the mountain, leading an old horse with a load on its back. He had two children with him, possibly six and eight, each carrying a load. She reached over to the director, touched his arm, and pointed to the family. Quickly, he grabbed a nice doll and a big truck, ran over, and gave them to the niños and shook hands with the padre. Their appreciation left everyone with a truly good feeling. That was Christmas for all.

Chon's grandkids didn't have a tree. Louise offered, but they really didn't care for one. They had tamales, and that was Christmas. Irma and her husband had just bought a home and were very proud of it. The floor was still dirt, but someday they would have cement. The working restroom sat outside on a cement slab and was walled in with brick. It was a little more than three feet square and stood about three feet high. Louise had to use it. She looked around at the neighborhood and didn't see an audience, so she proceeded. She did wonder if they used an umbrella in case of rain.

Fences were clotheslines, and dishes were limited. Irma was especially pleased with her outdoor stove, molded from clay so that she had a flat top with different heats and two ovens. A canopy over the top kept the sun off. She was also excited over her new job, working three days a week in one of the clothing factories. They had given her a mug which she, with great pride, presented to Louise for Christmas.

Louise and Chon had taken the boys a soccer ball, and the entire neighborhood gathered for the big game with the new ball. Irma had prepared a washtub full of tamales, traditionally wrapping them in banana leaves. It was a good afternoon. That evening, Louise and Chon drove back to Tela with a pot full of delicious-smelling tamales, Chon's favorite food.

During most of the year, her time was spent with organized groups, school, ATAN, and church; but the week before Christmas was hers.

Several groups and churches in Lewistown sent her money. Off she went, to the city, and the *pulperìa* run by Maria's father where she ordered twenty big sacks of food. After that, she stopped at shops and sidewalk vendors to buy dolls of all sizes, cars, trucks, airplanes, and finally, apples. Navidad in Honduras meant apples and grapes, tamales, and family. If she ran out of gifts, an apple would always be a welcome gift.

Early on the twenty-fourth of December, she asked Carol and Chon to go with her. She couldn't manage the roads and paths with her leg. To be out there with all that food and those gifts was also dangerous.

She had picked a small barrio called *Quatro de Enero.*[47] She drove up to the houses; Carol and Chon handled the conversation and gave out food and gifts.

Poverty and hunger leaped out from the cardboard walls and lean-tos in the form of naked and shoeless children. The eyes were so wary, afraid of what these strangers wanted. Even poor and afraid, they were respectful and gracious.

---

[47]   Fourth of January

When the last bag had been handed to a teary mom with a new baby clinging to her hip, and the last toy and apple had been taken by happy children, they headed home.

"Thank you, Mrs. Langford," said Carol. "Thank you for letting me share this day. This is the nicest Christmas I have ever had." Even Chon nodded; the day had moved him too.

Carol had nothing. Louise knew, but she didn't say a word. That afternoon, I saw her take Carol three big sacks full of all kinds of food, complete with a large chicken, ready to be cooked. Carol looked into the bags and threw her hands up over her face, her big white eyes peeking through, and she giggled.

Christmas Eve could be so lonely. Louise often met Chon after Christmas Eve services and walked with the mariachi for a time.

They were passing the clinic late in the evening on this holiest of nights. A young mother and two children were huddled on the curb in front of the closed building. She was crying softy, holding her children close. Louise had a few toys in her car. She retrieved them and gave them to the *niños*, then handed the mother some money to get food. Christmas Eve was such a tragic time for heartbreak.

She went home after that—to spend the evening alone, as usual. Gaiety in the *cantinas* was at its peak on Navidad and busy for mariachis. She watched the neighbors welcoming family, hugs for all, happy chatter, grandmas exclaiming over how much the children had grown, and the fireworks a deafening blast from every street.

She was lonely, thinking of her children and their families, so happily enjoying each other and their Christmas traditions. It was hard not to be depressed. *Next year,* she thought. *Next year.*

CHAPTER 13

Louise began to study the Garifuna, descendants of the slaves who escaped the ships from Africa. They settled in villages up and down the north coast of Honduras, always living where the land meets the sea. Their culture and dances were carried from generation to generation, especially the *Janguru,* an extreme dance in masks and costume, performed by the men to frighten and ward off the slavers.

She first saw them on the beach, the black women walking in from the village. Their slow, easy gait was so relaxing to watch. The tubs on their turbaned heads were filled with either coconuts and a short machete or towel-covered coco bread, and they would stride along calling, "*Pan de coco. Pan de coco.*"[48] It was almost healing for a tired soul to watch these ladies, their large bodies swaying tirelessly along the avenue.

Many of the blacks still spoke their native African tongue along with Spanish, and many spoke English. Cornrows, usually complete with beads, adorned their thick black hair. Dancers performed in front of the beachfront hotels for crowds of tourists. Louise was totally in awe of them, but what really excited her were the drums.

She would watch their hands, so beautifully and skillfully drawing out the rhythm—rhythm that would not let you stand still. It tugged at your hips and shoulders, and your cares soared away. Only the music and rhythm mattered. It was fast. Dancers' bodies exploded with movement,

---

[48]   Bread of coconut

their tops still, but the feet and legs keeping an unreal tempo. Crowds formed wherever drums could be heard. These natives talked with their drums, in so many ways.

She heard it one evening about seven o'clock—a soft faint drumbeat, and then another, slow and soothing. She knew what it was. She got up from correcting papers and went to the front door where she could see straight down the street. People were gathering around Doña Chìla's house on the corner, one block up.

She had seen the old woman a week before. Carol told Louise the power to Doña Chìla's house would be cut because of her unpaid bill. Doña Chìla was a black who had no children of her own, but every hungry or homeless child in the area knew her name. They were always welcome, and many times her house was overflowing.

She had diabetes, and her leg turned bad. Louise gave Carol the money with the stipulation no one know where it came from—just a friend.

Now, as people gathered, the drums kept their vigil. Louise went up the stairs to the balcony where she could watch the small cement-block house on the corner and the people that clustered in little groups. She waved to her neighbor, Fatima, as she passed by; then she sat back, listened, and watched.

The drums never stopped. Sometimes it was one, sometimes it was more, but the rhythm was always the same—slow, melancholy, drawing and relaxing. Often, one or two Garifuna would stand and gently sway in time to the beat, their bodies in constant movement to the rhythm. Little fires had been lit in the garden, and they danced around them. Radios and televisions in the area were silenced. The drums talked all night; quietly, respectfully, sadly—filling the air with the news that Doña Chìla had died.

People sat, listened, and remembered. Sleep came and went, and the drums continued. At sunrise, they put the white sheet in the back of the pickup, and then Doña Chìla. They took her back to the village, back to her roots for her last rites. A strange sense of fulfillment, yet emptiness, engulfed the little barrio.

It was Sharlene, who had lived behind Louise in the cabañas on the beach, that first brought her deeper into the Garifuna culture. As a baby, Sharlene, who was black, had been adopted by a Scandinavian couple in Montreal, Canada, where she was raised. She was tall, strong, athletic, always happy, and walked with the regal stride of her ancestors. She and Louise had become good friends, despite the fact that she was younger even than Louise's children.

When Sharlene came to Honduras, she unknowingly walked straight into her roots. She earned her master's degree on her study of how the lands of the indigenous were being usurped by other agencies—a point of much controversy at that time.

She traveled alone into the primitive Mosquitia area, flying into an airstrip east of La Ceiba, then being taken by *cayuco*[49] deep into the swampy jungle, a journey of several days. She lived in a hut among the natives and learned their dialect and lifestyle.

Her months there, along with weeks of digging into dusty records in Tegucigalpa and San Pedro Sula, led to her final degree and the title of Dr. Sharlene Mollett, along with a professorship at Dartmouth.

The blacks clung to their heritage and became a tight-knit society; but here again, poverty and a rampant HIV took its toll. Medical personnel worked long and hard to contain the epidemic, which was well into the heart of the entire country, affecting not only blacks, but the light-skinned, the Indians, people from the mountains, the cities, and the farms. It is a battle still being fought, even now.

---

[49]   canoe

Louise loved the common people, the ones from the little aldeas, *campos*, and the villages. Often, when she needed to clear her mind, she would climb on the chicken bus—one that stopped every mile or so and carried everything, including chickens. She watched the folks interact, and often a young woman with a new babe would drop her blouse to nurse the child, covering her exposed shoulder with a thin blanket. It would be quiet, all eyes on the gentle scene, the mother's long dark hair falling over her shoulders and her eyes on the little bundle she cradled. The scene was so simple, so basic. In her mind, Louise recorded these memories, complete with the machetes lying on the floor and the old bus bumping along.

When it was time for mom and babe to get off, there were arms to help with every step. She was special; she was theirs.

Evenings brought relaxation, music, meeting friends at a restaurant, enjoying the quick sunsets—it was a time to forget work, cares, and to sit and visit with neighbors. For the women in the barrio, it was a time to gather at some intersection, set their plastic chairs together, talk and laugh, discuss the important local happenings, and recall the joys of the day.

While they talked, they used their towels to flick away the mosquitos, automatically shifting their chairs to dodge the smoke coming from small fires of burning coco shells or leaves, which were lit to dissuade the hordes of insects that appeared like clouds, bringing the dreaded dengue fever.

Not much escaped these ladies; news came from taxistas, deliverymen, or vendors. Ears were always open, and news traveled incredibly fast.

Women in the barrio were important to Louise. Thursday night was women's prayer night in Monte Fresco. Televisions were turned off at 7:00 p.m. The women passed down the lane to one of their houses, carrying a chair under one arm and their Bible under the other. They often invited Louise, but she said her Spanish wasn't good enough, so she would just listen.

Soon the clapping began, keeping time to the singing, happy and sad. Sometimes they cried and sometimes they laughed. They talked and told stories. It was their time, and no one interfered.

Their day began at four in the morning, the sound of their washboards echoing through the early silence. And the *slap-slap* of the tortillas, which grew larger with each pass to the other hand, readied everyone for the mouthwatering aroma that floated through the air as they cooked.

Louise had tried to make them, tried over and over, but hers were hard and oddly shaped. She threw them out. Even the dogs wouldn't eat them, burying all her efforts in the garden. She would get totally frustrated and asked Carol, "What do I do wrong?"

Carol would laugh and say, "Mrs. Langford, it must be the difference of our skin. Don't worry. One of these days, you will do it." I watched her practice, trying to master something that looked so simple. She never did.

Passing by her gate after Louise had finished washing, her neighbor ladies would often smile and say, "More shoulder, Miss, more shoulder."

These wonderful women cooked and cleaned from early morning until sunset. Now, on Thursday, these few hours belonged to them.

On a noisy, explosive New Year's Eve, a great commotion came from her gate, with people frantically screaming her name. "Teacher!" another neighbor, Marianne, called. "Please, Miss, we need you to take Maria to the hospital."

Louise grabbed her keys and ran out, asking, "What's wrong?"

"She drank some dog poison. She was jealous because her husband was talking to another woman."

Louise backed the pickup out. Juan ran up, carrying his wife, Maria, climbed in the front and held her as they started toward the city. She drove as fast as she could, Juan screaming at her all the time, "Go faster! *Mas rapìdo! Mas rapìdo!*" Maria would choke, and blood would shoot from her mouth.

"Hurry, Teacher, hurry!" She raced up the never-ending street, down the highway for another mile, through the big gate, and into the hospital grounds. Juan leaped out and carried Maria into the big door under the light. Louise waited.

Back he came, running. "Quick, Teacher, to the pharmacy. They don't have the medicine here." There was always one pharmacy in the city that stayed open all night.

The pharmacy had the medicine, but he had no money. Louise did.

Maria lived. It took a while, but she made it through. Her husband left and went to live with his other woman, and Maria survived the loss.

The need for help came again that holiday season. Money was needed two doors down when the woman's husband was shot four times at a party on New Year's Day. After that, the poor woman collected wood for her outdoor stove and baked *pastelitos*[50] to sell throughout the barrio. Louise liked her. She was quiet and hardworking—very hardworking. Louise also loved the pastelitos.

There were many trips, one to take Carol's daughter-in-law to the hospital to have a baby. The hospital, suspecting a cesarean birth, sent the girl sixty miles to San Pedro Sula to another hospital where nobody was allowed in. The staff came out to post births every few hours. Relatives clung to the wire fence waiting for word.

The labor rooms were packed to the extent two women shared a bed. Janine was extremely uncomfortable, so she lay on the floor. They forgot her, and she had no food for two days. Carol set up a huge fuss outside. The nurses finally found Janine under a bed. The cesarean section

---

[50]   Folded corn tortilla with meat filling

was performed that morning, and she came home the next evening. Louise took diapers, blankets, socks, pins, shampoo, powder, etc., to the beautiful baby girl. Other than what Carol had made her, Janine had very little.

There was another trip to San Pedro Sula to fix a grandma's broken arm, a ride which proved to be unreal. Her family was packed in the backseat and the box in back. They were all shouting directions to Louise in Spanish. A suspecting taxista stopped her, asked where she was trying to go, and had her follow him. Driving in San Pedro Sula literally meant taking your life in your hands.

If she needed information quickly, Louise learned to ask a taxi driver. If he didn't know, he would ask another, and soon someone would drive up with an answer. If she took the same taxi from the same spot twice, she could expect to see him waiting the next day. This was their world. They ruled it and held the power. Keeping their respect and support was important.

Most taxistas were honorable, but there were a few who weren't.

Louise saw the taxi, but too late. She had pulled out into the main street when she thought no one was coming. And then there he was.

She knew she was going to hit him. He didn't swerve, just let her front right fender hit his front. True to her northern training, she got out, apologized, told him it was her fault, and asked him to call the police. He was astounded.

Someone on the sidewalk said, "No, Miss, just give him some money and he will go away."

She had been warned about those who would try to force her into an accident because she was from the north and rich. But she was in the wrong and at the taxista's mercy.

She told the onlooker, "No, that's not correct. Will you call them for me, please?"

The man shook his head but called.

An officer eventually came. He looked over the accident, which wasn't too bad. She saw him point to her skid marks and to the clear pavement back of the taxi—no marks. They conversed.

The officer came over to talk to her. She said the fault was hers. He put her in the passenger side of her pickup and got into the driver's seat. Evidently, he had never driven a stick shift. He started in low and continued there, the poor pickup grinding away.

She tried to tell him he had to shift down. He shushed her and held up a silencing finger. Two miles more and he pulled into the police station up on the hill where the dorms were. Police on duty cannot go home until their tour of duty is over. They stay in the barracks.

Luckily, she drew a rather intelligent sergeant. He talked with her best he could. She was scared, nervous, and her Spanish left her; but she made out what she thought he was saying and tried to answer. He frowned a lot.

The taxi driver ranted, waved his arms, and yelled. The sergeant asked her for her license and papers.

"They're in the pickup. I will get them."

"No! Your car is impounded."

"But my papers—"

He shrugged.

"Can you pay for repairs to the taxi?" the sergeant asked.

"Yes, of course," she said.

"Good. Then go find out the amount."

She was put in another car and taken to the body shop, along with the taxi, and given an estimate of two thousand lempira. Back they went to the station.

"Have you the money?" the sergeant asked.

"The money is in my house," she said.

"Very well." He gave her the keys, and the first officer she met went with her.

She drove two miles through the city, then to Monte Fresco. In the barrio, neighbors were watching as she came down the road to her house, fender crumpled and the officer riding beside her.

Buddy discouraged the officer, so he stayed in the pickup. She entered the house, touched my head as she passed me on her way up the stairs, and took two thousand lempira from her closet. Back at the station, she gave the money to the sergeant.

"My wages," the taxi driver wailed. He was milking it for all he could.

"How much do you make?" asked the sergeant.

"Two thousand limps a day," the taxista lied.

"How many days to fix the taxi?"

"Five days," said the driver.

The sergeant looked at her. About this time, Louise regained her senses.

She stood, drew herself up, and in her best Spanish, said, "With respect, señor, I have already paid a good price for the repairs. If this taxista earns two thousand lempira a day, you would have no police. They would all be driving taxis.

"I want to be fair and pay for damage I caused, but this is too much. I will give him five thousand lempira total. That is all. With respect, señor." And she smiled.

So did the sergeant. "Do you have the money with you?"

She swallowed. "No, it is in my house."

Again, he called the same officer and gave him the keys to the pickup. And again, she drove—through the city, back to the barrio, down the lane to the house. She took all her money and went back to the station. The neighbors were still watching.

The sergeant took the money and looked at the taxi driver. "That is all."

To Louise, he said, "Señora, you will appear before the judge tomorrow morning."

Her lawyer friend sought her out that evening. "Louisa, why didn't you send for me? People go to prison for that." She knew he was worried about her Spanish.

"I was fine," she said, not admitting how very frightened she was. She really didn't think they would put her in prison, although there were a few moments she wasn't so sure. She had heard about the women's prison. It was horrid, ugly, and something she wanted to stay completely away from.

He offered to go to the judge for her, but she refused. She paid her fine the next day when she appeared in court, then took her pickup to her next-door neighbor, Alfie, who repaired it.

Alfie always fixed her pickup. No matter what the problem, Alfie fixed it—along with her plumbing, electrical, anything that broke or didn't work.

He was especially good with autos and worked on many vehicles in back of his home. Louise told the people back in Montana, "If you can't have AAA, you need an Alfie." She paid him well, and when she had a problem, he always came to get her and her pickup, no matter where she might be.

Louise's bad knee was making it harder for her to drive the old pickup with its clutch; so Chon, Alfie, and Louise set off for San Pedro Sula to trade it in for something else. They picked out a little Kia that had been wrecked in the United States and reconditioned in Honduras. Instead of a title of ownership, she was given a certificate of destruction, meaning it could never be brought back into the United States. They really liked the car. It drove well, was roomy, and suited their needs perfectly.

No one ever saw the taxi driver again. He took the money, ditched the taxi, and left town.

CHAPTER 14

A phone call one afternoon in the spring informed Chon that his son, Marvin, had been shot and killed while walking home from work in the evening. He lived in a small town near San Pedro Sula, was just finishing school, and came twice a year to help Chon and Louise wash the big house. She paid him well, and he liked coming to visit. He was quiet, smart, respectful, and didn't drink, do drugs, or smoke. He was a nice person. It was a random killing—no reason. Chon left immediately. He was different after he returned.

There was no warning. It was four in the morning of May 28, 2009. Louise was suddenly thrown from one side of the bed to the other. She tried to turn back, only to be thrown completely to the opposite side. The beams of the house groaned and growled like a huge angry monster.

The clay roof slabs scraped against each other unmercifully, back and forth—grinding, grating. Suddenly, the entire house started rocking violently in a different direction, again and again. It seemed like it would never stop, over and over.

She tried to move, only to be jerked back and tossed again. *Dear Lord, please, won't it ever stop?* Suddenly, it slowed. It had been thirty-five seconds of terror. Then, as if not enough, it began once more. She slipped off the bed to the floor, expecting the roof and back of the house to come down at any second. She waited. It held. The rocking slowed again; it stopped.

Smaller shocks began. She made her way to the bathroom where there was more support. Over forty aftershocks followed. People from the barrio were running, screaming, out to the road, not noticing the big telephone poles and their maze of heavy wires swinging back and forth. There was total panic. They feared there would be another.

She hurried down the stairs, bracing herself with her arms in case of another quake, picked me up from the floor, sat me back on my little stool, and checked the birds. Chon had already come down and was sitting at the table, talking quietly on his phone. "No, no, I can't come. You will be all right. It is all over now. No, I can't. Not now."

She looked at him. She had overheard the woman's hysterical voice, pleading. The guilt on his face said it all. She was stunned; she couldn't think. There was nothing to say. She went back upstairs.

The earthquake caused a great deal of structural damage to the area but no deaths. Evidently, it was centered deep in the ground, from the fault that ran directly across the North Coast, out in the sea. Louise was no novice to earthquakes. They were common in Montana, but this was too big, too close, and—she found out later—registered 7.1 on the scale. But her house held. We were lucky that night.

In June, Louise left for the States and more knee surgery. She came back to us in October, so weak. I could see it was hard for her to walk, but she did. The heat was still intense. Chon was not happy. They tried to act the same as always, but she knew—her fears corroborated by Carol who heard it from the taxi driver, who heard it from the vendor of fish, who learned it from the men in the streets. He was drinking a great deal, and there were other women.

Louise stayed at the house, healing, until January and then went back to the school. It was hard, especially the stairs. She said it would get easier. It didn't.

Chon was coming home very late, always quiet and needing money. When she said no, it made him angry, and he wouldn't speak for days.

Early one afternoon, he arrived in an ugly mood. He had been drinking and was surly and argumentative—not like our Chon. I watched as he shouted and backed her into the computer table. Every bit of my stuffing was scared. My world was about to come tumbling down. When he threatened to throw the television down the stairs, she grabbed his arm.

"*Que pasa! Que pasa!*" he shouted. "*Nunca tocarme!*" (What goes! What goes! Never touch me!) His eyes were wide, irrational power pulsing through his body. He reached under his arm and pulled out his pistol. I heard her scream, "No, Chon. No!"

He waved his pistol, still ranting. She covered her face with her hands, forced herself to turn her back to him, walked as fast as she could into the little bathroom, and locked the door, for whatever good that would have done. She was confused, her mind racing. *Dear God, what has happened to him? Help me. What can I do?*

She waited for what seemed hours. Slowly, she inched open the door. Nothing. She crept to the top of the stairs. I wanted to tell her he had gone, but she soon learned that. He was ashamed.

She buried her head in my old fur and cried.

He sold the pistol that week, but the magic was gone. The fear had begun. A love had changed. The house was sad.

Wednesday was cleaning day, and Esmerelde—Louise's short, happy house helper—came down the stairs and told Louise she thought Chon's leg looked bad again. Louise started past me up the stairs.

Chon's voice boomed out, "No, es okay."

"Let me see, por favor."

"No, es okay," he growled again.

She looked anyway. It was black, hot, angry, and swollen so that the skin was tight.

"Chon, you need to see a doctor."

"No, just get the medicine again for now."

She filled the prescription, like she'd done many times before, and began the shots. Chon's medical life had been a series of catastrophes. His drinking has wrecked his liver and caused problems with his legs swelling. Many times, she had encouraged him to give it up, and he had honestly tried; but his good intentions and valiant efforts only lasted a few days.

A car accident during a mariachi serenade years earlier had gashed his leg and led to infection. Louise had driven him to the doctor's office. Chon asked Louise to wait outside. She was North American. Not only would they have been charged much more, but she might have had to take him to an expensive private clinic.

The doctor, not realizing Chon was a bleeder, had opened the leg. He quickly put a tourniquet around it and rushed Chon to the hospital. She saw their frantic exit and followed in her car.

When she got to the hospital, the bloody trail led to the surgical rooms. A male nurse stopped her, made her put on a gown, and handed her purse back to her. She walked into a room under the SURGERY sign. The table was short. Chon's head was hanging over the top, so she put her purse under it.

There were no nurses or assistants. The doctor took a cauterizing unit from the wall, dusted it off, and plugged it in. He sealed the wound, and a few days later, Chon had come home.

The next episode came early one morning when he told Louise he was going to die that day. He said he was spitting blood. She had him lie down, talked with the doctor, and made arrangements to cover her classes at school. When Dr. Christina saw him, he had almost no blood pressure. She told Louise to get him to San Pedro Sula immediately, to an address she wrote on a slip of paper.

The bus ride was long. Chon hardly moved. The minute they arrived, she got a taxi to take them to the clinic. He lay in the waiting room until she could produce five thousand lempira for his care. She had only three thousand with her. Dr. Christina called the clinic, accepting responsibility for the money, and they took him into surgery.

The doctor told her he was full of blood, that there was a rupture somewhere in his lungs (she couldn't understand the Spanish) and they would try to band it, but that he would not survive the night.

At midnight, his breathing slowed to almost nothing. She talked to him, made him move a little and talk, anything to keep him going—and at six the next morning, he was still alive.

The doctor made four more trips down Chon's esophagus, banding the rupture. Louise called his daughter Irma, who came with all the relatives. They brought their lunches, ate on the ground outdoors, and sat bouncing on his bed, introducing nieces and nephews he had never met. The nurses were greatly upset, as was Louise, so she shooed them out. That was the only time she ever saw Chon shed tears.

She took him home after that day, but she often wondered what would have happened if he had died. She would have been sitting on the curb with a dead body, waiting for a taxi, needing a way to get him back to Tela. Life is not easy in the third world, and she was learning how hard it can be for a stranger.

Chon said something smart to a friend in a cantina early one afternoon. The friend, who'd had too much to drink, broke his beer bottle, chased

Chon down the street, and sliced upward on his face with the broken bottle, taking the end and top of Chon's nose. Blood was everywhere. Someone called Louise to get to the hospital, fast.

They sewed up his nose, but with no end, and open, it was ugly. He had been a handsome man and a performer. This was devastating for him, and Louise felt his hurt. He was sent to the hospital in San Pedro Sula, where they grafted enough skin to make him look good.

With all that behind him, he still drank the beer—too much beer. Now here he was, with a dark red and black swollen leg, again. Friday, Louise gave him a shot before she left for school. At ten o'clock, she got a call.

"I don't think the shots are working," he said.

She left school and took him to the doctor.

"You need to go to the hospital. I can get you right in," the doctor told him.

"No! She can take care of me," said Chon emphatically.

"Very well." Turning to Louise, the doctor asked, "Can you give him the injections?"

She nodded, took the instructions and prescriptions for more medicine, and they went home.

Two days later, Valentine's Day, it was better. His color improved. He was happier, and they laughed and went out to sit on the porch.

"Look," he said.

A huge water blister had appeared above the ankle. As he touched it, liquid began to drain. Then another appeared, and then another. She grabbed towels to curb the flow.

Louise had undergone surgery for another total new knee just months before and knew how dangerous this could be. She needed to protect herself from this obvious infection.

Running to the store, she bought extra-large diapers, cut the elastic, and slid them under the profusely draining blisters, which had now covered his leg and were appearing above the knee.

He slept on a cot on the floor so he wouldn't contaminate the sofa and the bed, but it got no better. She battled it for another day, changing the dressing every hour. Carol suggested the hospital, but Chon said no. At school, the bookkeeper, Farida, talked to Louise. "Mrs. Langford, you need to take him to the hospital. If he dies in your house, you could go to prison."

That was a jolt. The leg worried her, but dying—*no!* In the evening, she thought she detected a faint odor from the leg.

Enough. She got Carol, who said it was late in the day. "Please, Carol, help me."

They went upstairs. Carol spoke to him. "Chon, we need to take you to the hospital. I think you have an infection."

"No, I'm fine!"

"Please, Chon, let us take you in to be checked," Louise said. "If they say you can come home, I will bring you right back." Looking back, she realized he must have known; he had to have known.

He finally agreed.

At the hospital, they put him in a wheelchair, and Carol wheeled him in. Louise sat in the car and watched. She could not be present or they wouldn't care for him; they would make her take him to a private clinic. There had been an auto accident and two shootings. The doctor and both nurses were working as fast as they could. Chon sat in the wheelchair for hours. Louise watched through the window. Near midnight, Carol came, got into the car, and said, "They've taken him."

Early the next morning, Louise took him a blanket, pillow, clothes, water, juice, and a toothbrush. He was very quiet. She removed his clothes. There had been no attention. A nurse came in and told her, "We need some medicine, and there is none in the pharmacy. You need to go to the city."

She left to buy the medicine. It was raining hard. Returning to the hospital, she set the little bottle on the bedside stand, patted his arm and said she would be back.

His daughter, Irma, and his brother from Yoro came to visit. Louise was relieved. She had been asking them to come for days. *Thank God they were there.* Since only one could visit at a time, she stayed at the house so they could spend time with him.

At 6:15 Thursday morning, I saw her gathering clean clothes for him and start for the stairs. Her phone rang. It was Irma.

"Louisa, *me poppy murier* (my father died)."

She sucked in her breath. "No, no. It can't be."

She clicked the phone shut, gasped, and sat down on the bed, unable to breathe. I could hear her fumble for water, then breathe again.

Coming down the stairs, she grabbed me, and sobbed in my soft fur. I heard her heart break, like so many times before—when she lost Lennie, after her mother died, and then Charley, her big bird—that deep sob that seemed to come from the depths of her soul.

Then she was out the door to get Irma and Chon's brother. She checked down the lane to see if Carol had left already. Seeing Janine, she told her what had happened and asked her to contact Carol. She needed her. On the way, she called the school. It was still raining.

At the hospital, she asked to see Chon.

"No!"

"Yes!" She had reached her limit.

They took her back to the morgue where he had been tossed on a tray and pushed back into the vault. She covered him as best she could and took his hand. It was still warm, but so limp and so dear.

A voice spoke behind her, "Teacher, if you go get a box, I will load him and come prepare him at your house. We can't do it here because of the infection. I live in Monte Fresco, you know."

"*Gracias.*" She left.

A box. Where would she go to get a box? Both Irma and Alberto were too upset to be of any use. Irma was dissolved into phone calls, and Alberto did not know Tela.

She needed money. That meant a stop to see Gabriel, the moneychanger on the street, who had been accepting checks from her bank in Lewistown. He was a large man, friendly, and cautious. He ran a high-risk business; moneychangers were killed every day in Honduras. She parked her car alongside the curb and waited for him to step up to her car window.

"Gabriel, I need money. Can you give me some?"

"Yes, Teacher. I heard about Chon. Whatever you want."

She wrote a check for what she thought would be enough. Gabriel used his hand calculator and quickly figured up the exchange rate, then handed her a bundle of money. The other two in the car stared at her.

Finally, she called Melvin, the sixth-grade teacher who had helped her many times.

"Melvin, I hate to bother you, but where do I go to find a box?"

"Stay there, Mrs. Langford. We'll be there to help you." And there they were—Melvin and Rev. Lone, with a healthy collection taken from the teachers and students.

They took three thousand lempira and instructed Louise to stay in the car, out of sight. Minutes later, they were back, carrying a black burial box. It looked small, but they both smiled and said he would fit.

The coffin was put in the back of the reverend's pickup, and he drove to the hospital. Chon was packed into the small box. Then they took him back to the house. By the time she arrived, friends had come, rugs were rolled up, chairs moved back, and a stand borrowed to hold the casket. Carol's daughter-in-law, Janine, had taken over. Louise asked about Carol. Janine simply shook her head. She said Carol must still be at work.

The mortician arrived with his helper. They looked at her, expecting her to leave. She shook her head, and they began to prepare and dress him. They simply laid his clothes on top of the body.

Louise gently moved them aside, took her scissors, cut the backs out of the necks so they would fit better, and tucked them in around him. Then they closed the lid. There was a window in the top for viewing, and she laid his big old guitar and his black hat on the other side.

Irma came up and took Louise by the arm. "The last thing my poppy said was 'I worry what will happen to my Louisà.'" Then she gave her a hug.

A mariachi friend came and began to sing to Chon. A neighbor lady asked for scissors and cut four bouquets, one for each corner of the box. People came, then more and more. Someone brought fifty chairs, and still it rained.

There was coffee, cake, rolls, sugar—so much. The school representation came and left, but no Carol.

Then someone told Louise, "The family is here." They came from the mountains, nineteen of them. They had traveled all day. The women wore towels over their heads and wailed. The men were silent and did not smile.

Motioning for Louise to open the casket, they examined Chon, nodded, and she replaced the lid. After a little while, as they were standing at the casket looking at Chon, his older brother told stories to Chon's twin sister, Pura, and they all listened and smiled. The stories were good.

Louise gave Pura a dark *pareja*[51] to wrap around her instead of the wet towel.

It got to be late, and everyone was hungry. Louise had not thought of that. Esmerelde came in, and Louise mouthed "help." Dear Esmerelde dove right in and made a big kettle of chicken soup. A huge pot of rice and veggies, traditional food, arrived from Isa and Giovanni's hotel. Again, Louise looked for her friend Carol. Where was she?

More people came; several were sitting and visiting on the stair steps. Louise finally pushed by a neighbor and went up to lie down a few hours.

I had a good view of everything from my stool on the stairs and watched the others mourn and talk. All Chon's children were there, half sisters and brothers, some meeting for the first time; children from different families and parts of Honduras. They visited the entire night.

In the morning, Chon was taken to the Milagrosa Catholic Church for the funeral. The Episcopalian minister, Rev. Lone, drove his pickup with Chon's casket resting on a white sheet in the back, surrounded by flowers, his brothers and sons riding on either side.

In the church, Louise looked around. Her senior class was standing behind her, as well as many of the parents. School had been dismissed. She was overwhelmed with emotion.

---

[51]   stole

After the service, Chon was again loaded into the back of the reverend's pickup for one last trip through the streets he had walked every day, on to the cemetery, and then carried to his final resting place near the very top of the mountain.

The sun appeared, and the seniors helped Louise up to the gravesite. The gravediggers had not yet finished, so the mourners sat in the sun and watched as the men would shovel more, get down and measure with their string, then shovel some more. She asked Melvin to give a little prayer. It was an extremely long, little prayer. Melvin was a minister as well as a teacher.

She saw his brothers talking, concern on their faces. It was very hot, and they were worried about the casket. Louise was sitting next to it. They came over to her, gently moved her back, then took hammer and nails and nailed the coffin lid closed. Finally, the workmen stepped back. The family gathered around, circling his grave, and Chon was put to rest covered with flowers from his garden.

The family was taken to the bus, given fare to get back home, and Louise, alone, drove back to her house. It was two o'clock. Her friend was still not there. Janine looked at her, reading her thoughts, and sadly shook her head.

Edna and Maria, both neighbors, had stayed at Louise's and not gone to the funeral. The house was clean, rugs and furniture back in place, the cement washed, chairs returned—everything done, as though nothing had happened. In thirty hours, her world had changed.

The two ladies took Louise to a little bush, not two feet from where everyone had been sitting under the carport, and there in the tiniest of nests was a mother hummingbird covering her little baby. *How frightened she must have been,* thought Louise.

The white sheet that lined the pickup with the casket to the church and the cemetery was later put into the tubs of Clorox, with all the towels that had been near the infection. They were soaked for days, washed with strong soap, aired, and given away.

Carol's absence bothered Louise. They had been so close. She felt abandoned. After two days passed, she climbed into the car and drove the block to the corner, then turned to the right, drove down the lane, and parked in front of Carol's home. Her friend was on the porch, watching her.

Louise motioned with her arm. "C'mon."

Carol sat a moment, looked down, then got up. She carefully came down the broken steps and opened the door.

"Carol, please get in. Have I done something wrong?"

"Oh, Miss," she started, eyes brimming. "No, my friend, it isn't you. I walked to the corner and turned to your house so many times. So many times. But my legs just wouldn't go. I tried and they wouldn't move."

Her eyes were big, round, and immediately Louise knew. Carol had always hated death—a fear that wouldn't permit her to go to a funeral, superstition so deeply ingrained she would panic at the talk of death and turn the other way. She would sing in the procession and stand at the cemetery, but she could not be near a body. Louise used to remind her, "Someday it will be you or yours, Carol. You have to get over this fear."

Louise reached out and touched Carol's arm. "I understand. How about a Coke on the beach?"

She put the car in drive, and they set out for the city. As they passed Janine's house, she saw a smile on the daughter-in-law's face. All was good again.

Support came from many special North American teachers she had met during her years at the school, bonds forged that would last a lifetime. Her friend, Jean Valentine, called from Texas with encouragement and love. They visited as old friends do. Another caller told her Jean closed her phone after talking to Louise, started to walk back across the room, and dropped dead from a heart attack.

CHAPTER 15

Chon died in February.

The teacher was alone now and coped well, but she was cautious and alert. She was afraid after Chon died. So vulnerable out there on the edge of town, she worried about the gangs of young men moving into the country, accompanied, as always, by drugs.

She returned for classes that next week and, within a month, knew she could not return for another year. She gave her final notice, firmed with a letter to the bishop, and it was done.

Late one night, when it was dark, something dropped on the balcony. From where I sat in the stairwell, it sounded like rope. Louise heard it too. She shined the flashlight all over but didn't see anything.

The next day was Sunday. She got up, fed the palomas who roared in sounding like a helicopter, swirling about her hair and arms as she made her way to throw the corn on the carport roof. After she fed the birds, she went to the computer table to check on her e-mail, paying little attention to the larger than normal bunch of cords piled underneath. Then down the stairs with the little red-and-black rugs she had braided for each individual step. Finally, after several more trips up the stairs, she left for church.

It was noon and stifling hot when she got back. She parked the car outside the gate, greeted the dogs on her way in, dropped her purse on the couch, and sat down at the table below the stairs. Taking a glass of cold water from the refri, she returned to her seat and began thumbing through the new Avon catalog, Spanish version.

Her chair was directly under the open steps of the stairway and next to Dorilla's cage. As she sat there, something caused her to look up. I heard her describe it later:

"I was totally engulfed in a most peaceful, tranquil aura, like being inside a huge bubble.

"There was light, but from no special place. It was so clear and bright. I just felt this inexplicable peace. Something spoke to me. There were no words. It was as though a thought entered my brain, but the words were there. *No matter what happens, you will feel no pain. You will not hurt.*"

A second later, this reverie—or whatever it may have been—was shattered by the lock clanking on the gate. She hesitated. She wanted the peace back. It was so glorious. Even bringing it to mind put her back in that presence.

Carol's "yoo-hoo" called again. She sighed and rose to go to the door.

"Come in, Carol. Let's have some tea."

"Annie said you were looking for me." Annie was Carol's daughter.

Louise frowned. "I haven't seen Annie, but come on in."

They drank tea, talking and laughing. Carol was always happy. Black, chunky, and good-natured, she could verbally put a sailor to shame when she got angry. Her Spanish was good, fast, clear, and her vocabulary extremely complete in all areas. A good friend to Louise, she always respectfully called her "Mrs. Langford," or "my friend."

"It was so wonderful," Louise continued, trying to tell Carol what had just happened to her. "The most complete feeling of peace. This extraordinary quiet, bright sensation of total peace, as though nothing could hurt me—as though nothing mattered."

Later, Carol said she had to go. I had been listening and watching from my stool and wanted to call out, *No, no, don't go. She needs help.* I could see up those stairs, and it was bad, so bad; but I was only able to sit there, silent and helpless.

As she stood, Louise glanced at Dorilla's cage and cried, "Dorilla! Carol, help!"

Poor Dorilla was flat on the bottom of her cage, eyes open, wings spread, unmoving. I saw Louise reach in, take her out, hold her close until her little heart settled down, and then gently put her back.

Paco was also down but got right up. After the birds were settled, the two friends talked a few moments, wondering what had happened.

Walking to the door, she mentioned to Carol, "I have some things for you upstairs. Do you want to take them today or later?"

Carol, always eager to get school material, said, "Let's go."

They passed me sitting there on the landing and started up the stairs. Louise was pointing to some pictures hanging on the wall. "I think I'll take this one and this one, but I have to leave this and—"

"Stop, Mrs. Langford! Don't look up!" Carol shouted. "Come down! Hurry! Don't look up!"

Louise didn't look up. From where I sat, I knew what must have been racing through her mind, hoping against hope it couldn't be. She knew and braced her body for the hard, swift bite she instinctively knew would come. Going down was so slow, one step at a time with her bad knee. It seemed like an eternity.

Finally, five steps down, Carol spoke. "You're okay. Relax." She raised her arm, pointed up the stairwell, and said one word, "Coral."

There he was; his ugly blunt nose had been just inches from Louise's head when Carol saw him. The top half of his dark red-and-black-banded body was flailing through the air, looking for a secure spot to grasp on to. He was big, old, deadly, and had been hiding behind a large Mayan mask carved out in the back, the spiral eyes busy, hypnotizing, with the moving coils behind.

Louise stood for a moment, unbelieving, and then started for the machete.

"No," Carol said. "You watch him. I'll get Alfie."

As is so true in some of the worst scenarios, a little humor creeps in. She ran next door. I heard her knock, and then again.

"Good morning, Carol." Fatima was tall, dark, pretty, with snappy black eyes. She was also a teacher, but in the government schools.

"Good morning, Fatima," Carol returned.

Proper salutations! Even at the most distressing times, Hondurans always give proper salutations.

"How are you today, Carol?"

"Fine, Fatima, and you?"

"I'm well. What can I do for you?"

"Is Alfie here?"

"Just a moment." Turning, she called toward the back rooms. "Alfio!" Then again, "Alfio!"

"Yes?" came an answer from the back of the house.

"Teacher Carol needs you."

Alfie appeared in the hall. He was tall, muscular, Italian, and very handsome. "Hello. What can I do for you?"

"Alfie, Mrs. Langford has a big coral snake in her house, and we need help. Can you come?"

"Just let me get my shirt and I'll be there. My cousin is here. I'll bring him."

All this time, the snake was winding around the pictures, in and out, hanging down over the stairs where Louise sat earlier looking at the booklet. As she watched, her thoughts went back to that morning—of Dorilla flat-bottomed from fear and the words she had heard: *Don't be afraid, you will have no pain. You will not hurt.*

And then Carol, Alfie, and his cousin were in the door. Buddy and Igor miraculously sat and watched them come in without a questioning growl.

Alfie pinned the snake's head down with his machete, grasped it from behind with his hand, and took all four-plus feet of red and black ugliness outside. There he decapitated it and threw the rest across the road for the chickens and ants to feast on.

Louise said that where she came from, there were always two snakes if there was one; so Alfie and his cousin looked all over the house, but it was clear.

Carol looked at Louise and said, "He was this far from your head," and showed her three inches between her fingers.

Louise talked to her friend quite a bit after everyone left. She could visualize Him smiling and saying, "Trust me, Louise. Trust me."

I knew she was still bothered because when she went to bed, she checked all over the rooms, left every light on, and kept looking across at the mask on the wall above my little stool.

She finally got out of bed, carefully took down the mask as though expecting something to jump out, put it in a large plastic bag, looped the top, and sat it out on the balcony. Way out. Then she went back to bed and tried to sleep sitting up, with all the lights on, so she could see any wiggles crossing the floor.

It was never going to get easier. She had just passed another birthday, and that was yet another reason she decided to give up this beautiful piece of paradise—its orchids, gentle breezes, bushes of fragrant jasmine, ginger flowers, bougainvillea, clouds of orange and yellow blossoms, the purple wisteria, those huge pots she had so happily collected on trips with Chon and Carol, her beloved Dorilla, Paco, Buddy, Igor, and the chicks and palomas—all her little bit of heaven.

But the ache for her children, her need for family and her country, and the loneliness all rushed onto her. So when a couple came to look at the house and agreed to her low price, she hugged me, cried, caressed my old woolly head, and put me into a box headed for home in Montana, and the cold.

CHAPTER 16

Lupè was one of the first people she met when she came to Tela. The last time Louise saw her friend was when she went to tell her good-bye. She found her outside the little house. Lupè walked up to the car window, and Louise asked, "Have they found Donaldo?" Lupè's son had been missing for several weeks.

"No, Miss, but I know he is dead."

"Have you called the police?"

"No, Miss, I think it was the police who did it."

Louise knew he was dead. She had talked to someone who had seen his body.

"Miss," Lupè said, "don't get out. They are watching us. They have lists. You have to leave . . . now. Just smile and wave. I love you, Miss."

Louise smiled, swallowing the lump in her throat. For seventeen years Lupè stood by her and supported her, and now she had to leave her like this.

Waving good-bye, she backed the car out, and when she saw a group of young men on the corner, watching, she forced a smile, nodded hello, then pulled into traffic, her heart thumping. She knew Lupè's son was at one time involved in drugs. In Honduras, that wasn't hard. Now the kidnappings and shootings had begun, escalating each day and for no reason.

She had taught for two weeks with guards and guns outside her class. The son of a factory owner had been kidnapped and a threat made against his brother, one of her pupils. It all ended well, and the brother returned after a healthy ransom was paid.

By 2010, *La Prensa*'s front pages were covered with pictures of bodies, bound and shot gangland style. Kidnappings had increased, businessmen were being assassinated in their cars, news reporters were shot on the streets, and buses were stopped, the passengers robbed and often shot and killed. On one Christmas Eve, a drug-happy gang massacred an entire busload of men, women, children, and babies. The world never learned of the bloodbath.

Gangs and drugs had overtaken that dear country. People were afraid . . . again.

I saw and heard about the final farewell. Parents and students from so many years were not about to let her just fade away. The cultural center was opened. Students came home from colleges. Others who had left the school joined their old friends and classmates, retired teachers, and grandparents. Reunited families and friends hugged and clasped hands.

A dance troupe wowed everyone with their fire dance, the dance of the bulls, the machete dance, and finally the grand Honduran folk dances with their magnificent costumes. It was fantastic. The troupe included one of her taxi drivers, one of the tellers in her bank, and the leader was her next door neighbor, the one who had owned the billiards.

She was presented with a huge hand-carved mahogany plate, engraved on the back. Students performed and photos shown on an overhead screen made a special night into history. There could have been no finer farewell.

As she left the house for the last time, she didn't look back. A piece of her heart was back there.

Buddy and Igor were buried in back of the house they protected. She and the vet had put them down the day before. Old and sick, they could never have adjusted to being with someone else. It was the kindest thing she could do, but it tore her to pieces. A block to the right, in the little cement house with flowers on the porch, was her beloved Dorilla, in her new home with Carol.

She kept her eyes ahead. She saw people gathered in small groups waiting to say good-bye. Emotions choked her.

"Good-bye, Miss."

There were tears, hands reaching in through the back window of the taxi to grasp hers, pulperia owners rushing out to join the others, saying *"Adios, vaya con Dios"*[52] and wishing her well.

On to the little bridge over the creek that separated the barrio of Monte Fresco from the city, the little bridge where robbers would wait for the big delivery trucks. She smiled. She had escaped that one. They drove to the city, past the school, and over the big bridge—so full of memories— and down to hotel Caesar Mariscos for the night. *Tomorrow . . . home. Oh, the thought of it!*

I did hear, from my big box in the corner of her room at Candy's, that her trip to the airport was a horribly unnerving experience.

Louise and Miguel, her taxi driver, left Tela early the next morning. Good-byes had been said, and she was ready, wanting to get to the airport before the crowds, make sure everything was in order, and rest for the trip home.

When the Honduran people have problems with government, problems that refuse to be addressed, they resort to severe actions, such as roadblocks. Set up at strategic points, they completely stop any vehicle

---

[52]   "Good-bye, go with God."

movement on the roads with no exceptions. Ambulances, fire trucks, school buses—nothing moves. Anyone trying to walk across the line to the other side is stoned from a huge truck filled with rocks at the center of the roadblock. It stays this way until demands are met.

Just outside Progreso traffic slowed and finally stopped, with Louise's taxi directly behind a double-long, open semi filled to capacity with oranges. It was early and truckers were trying to get their produce delivered before the sun got higher. Cars were stopped for miles. Word came down the line. Miguel leaned in the taxi window and shook his head.

"Roadblock, Miss. Sorry. I hope you don't miss your plane."

"What's the reason for the roadblock, Miguel?" she asked.

"It's the nurses and teachers. They haven't been paid for six months."

She called her ticket agent. There was nothing to do but wait. Her cell phone was nearly dead and wouldn't last.

Three hours passed. She needed a restroom. It was ungodly hot, especially sitting in the taxi. Thankfully, she had a full water bottle. She was never without water. And there were always oranges; the hot sun was literally cooking them, and the smell was getting pretty strong. People milling around were encouraged to help themselves to the sweet, juicy fruit.

Finally, the line moved, but just a few feet; then another six or seven. Stop. There was no time left. If they were clear now and drove at top speed, they would barely make the flight. The battery in her cell phone was dead.

Then, incredibly, the line began to move again, but so slowly, passing though double lines of riot police sent by the government. They wore the black helmets, heavy black padded body vests, and carried riot guns and the big shields.

It was zero tolerance, and she knew what that was. She had seen it during Semana Santa, when thousands went to Tela to spend Holy Week at the beach. It meant they could throw you in jail for any reason, even if they thought you were doing wrong, and you stayed there under inhuman conditions until the judge felt like seeing you or you could buy your way out. This last option made outsiders easy prey and worried Louise.

As they came to the city of El Progreso, she couldn't resist. She raised her camera and snapped a picture of the police on the left. It was a bad move. As she put the camera down, the police moved in front of the taxi and pointed to the side of the road. She was worried—really worried.

Miguel pulled over and stopped. Policemen threw open both front doors and motioned them out. She stepped out of the taxi and reached for her purse.

"No," the officer shouted and motioned her back away from the taxi. All her papers were in her purse. She wanted to argue, but one look from the officer stopped her. Two more policemen ran up and surrounded the car, shouting.

One bent down and reached under the front. He pulled a burning piece of rubber tire from under the left front of the taxi, then waved them back into the car and walked away.

Tickets were being written and passed out to cars that tried to jump the line or take shortcuts through the city. There was no time. Each minute was so important to make that flight. Now, it seemed there was no hope.

Down to the wire, they passed a side road that led to the main highway and the airport. Miguel looked at her, eyebrows up. She nodded. He swerved and drove at breakneck speed through four-way stops and across intersections, not daring to slow until they got to the highway, then racing for the airport. She wouldn't let herself think what might have happened if someone had been crossing their path.

At the airport, Miguel slid to a stop directly in front. She dashed to the counter. It was closed. She yelled and cried, joined by a man who had also just arrived. Together, they set up a ruckus, yelling and banging on the counter. A clerk finally came out, and after much more talking, yelling, and tears, he talked to someone else then came back.

"How fast can you run?" he asked.

"I can't," she replied.

"Try."

They dashed through the first security, up the stairs into the checked security. Miguel had somehow seen that her one suitcase and carry-on were with her.

Off with her shoes, open her bag, hurry, hurry—no time to snap shoes.

"Hurry, ma'am. They're leaving."

She was running, trying not to fall and to keep her shoes on. From out of nowhere, a wheelchair appeared. It came up behind her, touched her knees from the back, and she fell into the chair. It turned, shot backward, whirled again, and dumped her into the plane.

"My suitcase!"

"It's in the compartment above your seat."

She sat down in 11C as the plane was pushing out. She was still silently crying, totally wrung. Her heart was thudding. *This wasn't how she wanted to leave. Dear God. But she was safe and going home. Thank you.* There was no possible way she could have made that plane without Him, and she knew it.

Hours later, after regaining her composure, she realized they should be nearing the mainland. She began watching out the little window, scanning the horizon, looking for something very dear and important to her. She leaned forward, straining to see.

There it was, flying high over the Houston airport—that beautiful big flag, stars and stripes waving majestically in the wind, beckoning to her, welcoming her home.

As usual, when she saw it, tears welled in her eyes and then slid down her cheeks. She thought of the little flag she had carried for seventeen years pressed between the last two pages of her daily journal. *She was home. Dear God, she was home.*

She had opted for a wheelchair because of her knee, and as they wheeled her in front of the immigration officer, she handed over her papers and passport. The officer was young, short, with long dark hair. She looked at Louise, saying, "I see you are in and out of Honduras quite a bit."

Louise knew where the agent was going; drug running was at an all-time high. She answered, "Yes, I taught English in a bilingual school in Tela, Honduras. It's been seventeen years, and I'm finally coming home." The day's emotions caught up with her, and her voice broke.

The officer reached across the counter, took her hands, smiled at her, and said, "Welcome home, Mrs. Langford."

It took weeks for this last experience to lessen in her mind—months for the hurt, loneliness, sadness, and frustration of the past year to pass. As in all things, time did its healing. Louise spent precious days with each of her children and then took a retirement apartment back in Lewistown. I have my place on the bed, atop a wonderfully soft white quilt; leaning against five fluffy white pillows, a little *typico* Honduran pillow at my side.

Our seventeen-year odyssey is over, and we are happy. She says she's the most fortunate of women. She has lived different lives in different worlds, met unforgettable friends, raised the nicest of children, enjoyed grandchildren and great-grandchildren, and had the love of three wonderful men.

God has taken such good care of her all these years, and I'm glad.

I still get a smile from my Louisa and a pat on the head. And when she's sad, she holds me close.

Tela 17 19194

I Love you
Teacher
ELvira Marcela

ACKNOWLEDGMENTS

So many people had a hand in this manuscript. Getting started was a huge problem, but it was made easier by encouragement from Candy and my friend Ann. There to read the first pages, they were the ones who pushed me ahead, chapter by chapter.

Son Lew, who lived in Ohio, was always on hand to walk a not-so-savvy computer novice through hours of painstaking learning into the ways of Word. And finally, it was Lew who helped tear the manuscript apart, evaluate the contents, and revise it in a timely fashion. For that, I am so very grateful.

Granddaughter Meghan was always just a phone call away with an "I'll be right there, Grandma." A whiz at computers, she usually arrived just in time to save this frustrated old lady who could never seem to get out of the "typewriter age." She was a sweetheart who could always take a moment or so just to listen.

Thanks to Andre for stepping in and opening up the world of publishing and agents—a dog-eat-dog world not made for people my age. Her support and incentive were stimulating and inspiring.

Finally, to friends and family for reading, supporting, advising, and encouraging me to have it published even when I threatened to put it in the bottom drawer and forget it. To Dixie, Ramona, Ruth, Helen, Ann, Elizabeth, and family—Connie, Cindy, Candy, Meghan, and

Lew—who wanted this legacy for their children and grandchildren. My love and thanks to you all.

Lastly, but equally important, I need to thank Ben and the members of the Xlibris staff—a team of seasoned professionals who so masterfully put everything in order and produced this book. My gratitude.

INDEX

snakes, xi, xiv, xvi, 14, 22, 53, 70–72, 77, 83, 92–95, 152
soccer, 19–20, 54, 122
social security, 38–39, 41–42
spiders, 70–71, 93
students, xiv, xvi, 12–13, 17–21, 47, 61, 96, 102, 104–6, 112, 120, 144, 155
superstition, 147
Suzanne, 50

T

tarantulas, 14, 93–94
taxistas, 13, 26, 29, 42, 115, 127, 130, 132
teachers, 12, 15, 21, 23, 29, 144, 147, 155
Tegucigalpa, 8, 37, 41, 126
Tela, 1, 7–9, 12–13, 26, 34, 36–38, 40, 47, 54–55, 58–59, 62, 64–66, 73–74, 117, 121–22
Tessie (hen), 90–92
Texas, United States, 56, 147
third world, xv, 11, 22, 27, 57, 68, 101, 115, 139

tobacco, 32–33
Tom, 7, 39
Tornabe, 63
tortillas, 32, 77, 128
transitos, 9, 40, 117
Triumfo de la Cruz, 63
Tulepanes, 72

U

United States, 7, 9, 37–38, 40, 88, 102, 106, 112, 134
US embassy, 37–40

V

Valentine, Jean, xii, 68, 110–12, 115, 120–21, 147
Veronique, 26, 50
visas, 32, 37–38

Y

Yoro, 54–55, 72, 142

Printed in the United States
By Bookmasters